STARFOX ADVENTURES

Official Strategy Guide

By Doug Walsh

||||||BRADYGAMES®
TAKE YOUR GAME FURTHER®

CONTENTS

Due to the ongoing development of the game prior to the game release, there may be some slight differences between the screen shots shown in this guide and what appears in the actual game.

2

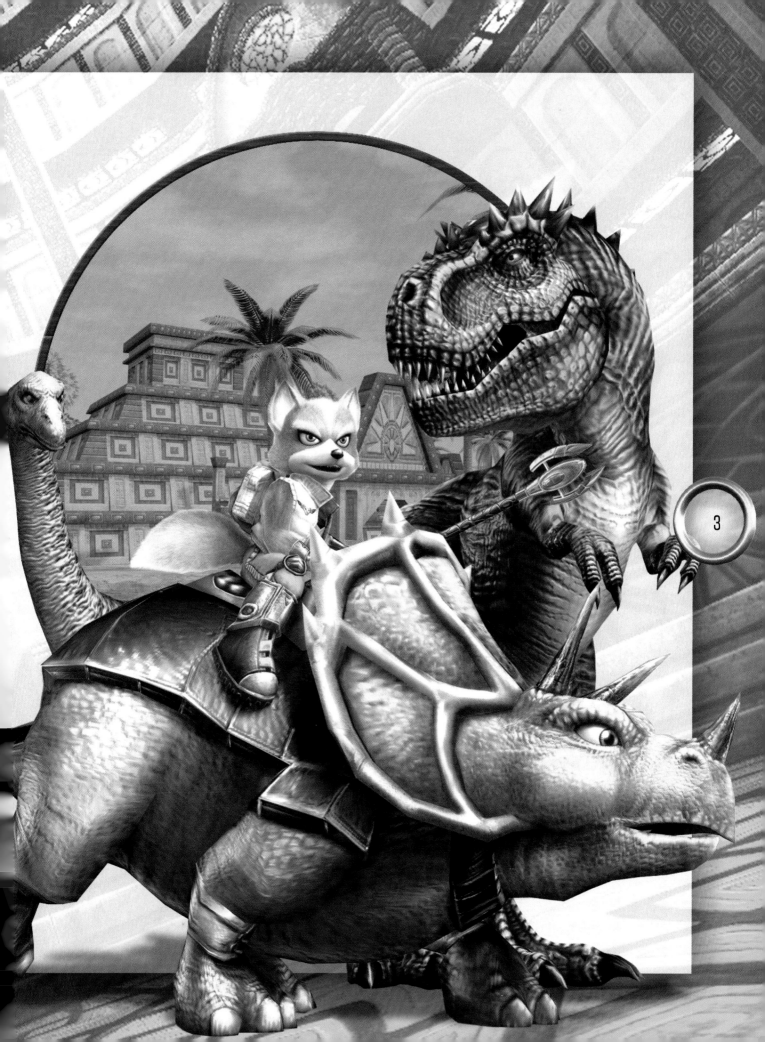

CHARACTERS

STAR FOX TEAM

FOX McCLOUD

Fox McCloud, leader of the Star Fox team and pilot of the Arwing, has grown a lot since his defeat of Andross eight years ago. His efforts to save the Lylat System have brought him great esteem throughout the galaxy. With the recognition comes greater responsibility. Although much of his time lately has been spent chasing after petty thieves, he still manages to devote a portion of each day to weapons and hand-to-hand combat training. Fox has developed into quite the martial arts expert!

4

PEPPY HARE

Peppy may have hung up his pilot's "wings" and retired from active combat, but he's still an integral part of the Star Fox Team. Peppy is now putting his years of experience to use as an advisor and navigator. Fox can count on him to provide up-to-date course headings throughout the game.

SLIPPY TOAD

Ever since the defeat of Andross, Slippy has had more time to devote to his true love—weapons research! Slippy is a self-admitted "techno-geek" and really enjoys his new role. His recent upgrades to the Arwing fleet and ROB the Robot have been greatly appreciated by the rest of the Star Fox team. Slippy can be relied upon for technological upgrades as well as important information and tips.

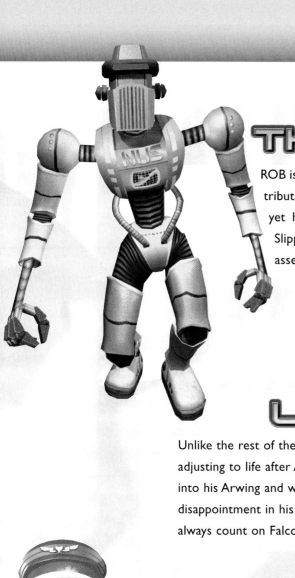

ROB THE ROBOT

ROB is Slippy's creation and is slowly starting to become a contributing member of the Star Fox team. Although ROB doesn't yet have as much personality as the other members, nor Slippy's love for rock n' roll music for that matter, he is an asset nonetheless.

FALCO LOMBARDI

Unlike the rest of the Star Fox Team, Falco had a really hard time adjusting to life after Andross. One day several years ago he jumped into his Arwing and was never seen or heard from again. Despite his disappointment in his friend's departure, Fox knows that he can always count on Falco to bail him out of a jam.

GENERAL PEPPER

Fox may be the leader of the Team, but even he takes his orders from someone; that someone is General Pepper. The General is responsible for contracting out projects that fit the skill level of the various space mercenaries. There's no team he likes more than Star Fox team! General Pepper may only appear as a hologram, but his tough-as-nails character comes across clear as day. Fox would be wise to do as he says, especially if he wants to get paid.

OTHER KEY PLAYERS

KRYSTAL

No one may ever understand the forces behind the destruction of Krystal's home planet, but it was definitely the power of fate that caused her path to cross with Fox's. Krystal doesn't speak English, but her ability to speak dinosaur may prove useful.

GENERAL SCALES

General Scales is the overlord of Dinosaur Planet and relies on brute force and intimidation to keep the various dinosaur tribes from rebelling. In the past, the EarthWalkers could keep him at arm's length, but not anymore. The General has found a way to make himself much stronger and is now bent on the destruction of his very own planet!

TRICKY

The young Prince Tricky isn't just the heir to the throne of the EarthWalker Tribe, but he may also be the very one who can rescue them from destruction. This spunky little dinosaur prides himself on the Sidekick Commands his father had taught him and is all too willing to use them.

DINOSAUR PLANET TRIBES

EARTHWALKER TRIBE

The EarthWalkers are one of the two ruling tribes on Dinosaur Planet, which gives them the edge in terms of respect among the other four-legged creatures. The royal family consisting of the Queen, King, and Prince Tricky make their home in ThornTail Hollow. Unfortunately, the bodies of most of the other EarthWalkers litter the halls of Krazoa Palace.

THORNTAIL TRIBE

These amicable creatures are the namesake for the Hollow that Fox uses as a base throughout this quest. The ThornTails aren't just friendly, but they are an excellent source of local knowledge too!

REDEYE TRIBE

The RedEye are the most fearsome of all dinosaur tribes. Fox won't be doing any talking with the RedEye as they tend to let enormous teeth do their talking for them! To make matters worse, General Scales has released them from EarthWalker control and set them free to run loose in the Walled City.

HIGHTOP TRIBE

This tribe may have the smallest population, but they make up for it in shear size! The HighTops were among the SharpClaw's first captives as their enormous size and strength makes them a formidable enemy. The slow-moving HighTops were imprisoned with little warning.

CLOUDRUNNER TRIBE

The CloudRunners are the only winged dinosaur tribe on the planet and have used this fact to lay claim to a share of the power. Although their heritage prevents them from being as jubilant as the EarthWalkers, they are always willing to lend a helping wing for the good of Dinosaur Planet.

SNOWHORN TRIBE

Generations of SnowHorns have made a living out of surviving the harsh conditions of Ice Mountain and SnowHorn Wastes. Unfortunately, General Scales has taken advantage of their renowned endurance and enslaved many of them in the DarkIce Mines. Fox must find a food source for these gigantic beasts so they can be of assistance.

LIGHTFOOT TRIBE

This tree-dwelling tribe enjoys their privacy so much they gated themselves off from the other dinosaurs. The LightFoot aren't nearly as trustworthy of newcomers as the others are and will certainly question Fox's intentions should he wander into their territory. Fox shouldn't be surprised if they force him to prove himself to them.

MISSION BASICS

Welcome to *Mission Basics*, the single best resource for learning all of the ins and outs to *Star Fox Adventures*. This chapter will provide the aspiring space mercenary all the training and essential knowledge needed to complete the mission at hand. Whether you're new to the Star Fox series or not, this is the first time Fox McCloud is venturing outside the Arwing and there's a lot to learn.

CONTROLS

Star Fox Adventures has two separate control schemes, one for controlling the main character, Fox McCloud, and the other for flying the Arwing. This section outlines the controls for Fox. Players looking for tips on flying the Arwing will find all they need to know in the *Piloting the Arwing* section.

FOX'S CONTROLS

⊙		Move the character and aim the Staff
⊕		Switch between P.D.A. devices
Ⓒ		Scroll through inventory items and commands
Ⓐ	Button	Attack, select inventory items and talk
Ⓑ	Button	Put away the Staff, cancel commands, and exit inventory menu
Ⓧ	Button	Somersault, evasive actions during combat
Ⓨ	Button	Assign Sidekick Commands, Staff ability or menu items
▭	Button	First person view
L	Button	Hold for force field protection or to guard in combat
R	Button	Press lightly to center camera, hold down to strafe
◯	Button	Brings up the Communicator.

WHAT ABOUT KRYSTAL?

Krystal doesn't have all of the abilities and functions as Fox does, but her basic movements and combat controls are identical to those listed above.

THE STAR FOX COMMUNICATOR

At practically any time during the mission, the player can press the ◯ Button and bring up the Communicator. This device allows Fox to check his status, inspect inventory items, and even receive hints and suggestions from his fellow Star Fox Teammates. In addition to being a place to save your progress and quit the game, there are three images of Fox's teammates, General Pepper, Peppy Hare, and Slippy Toad.

GENERAL PEPPER

By selecting General Pepper, the player can check their overall gameplay status. The screen will detail the percentage to which the player has completed the game, the overall time spent playing, the number of SpellStones and Krazoa Spirits found, and other measures of gameplay progress such as the number of Energy Badges and size of the Staff's power meter.

General Pepper's status screen can be flipped by hitting Left or Right with the . The reverse side of the screen contains Fox's entire inventory of items, Staff upgrades, and available Sidekick Commands. Use the ⬤ to select an item and press the Ⓐ Button to read its description.

PEPPY HARE

Peppy is the consummate navigator and has prepared an entire map of Dinosaur Planet for Fox to refer to. Although the names of the different areas will only appear once Fox has visited them, once there, Fox can use the Ⓐ Button to select a location and receive a brief description of it from Peppy.

The true benefit of this map comes from its built-in navigational assistant. Fox can refer back to the map at any time and the location he needs to travel to next will be blinking. This feature works well with Slippy's advisory screen. Push the Ⓒ Left or Right to see the number of maps in your inventory.

SLIPPY TOAD

There's not a whole lot that Slippy doesn't know, so it should be no surprise that he's Fox's best source of advice. Whenever stuck in a puzzle or unsure what the next course of action should be, consult Slippy. He'll be more than happy to provide some gentle hints and tips to help get you out of any jam.

COMBAT TACTICS

Fox may have wanted to bring his laser gun with him, but the Staff he finds in ThornTail Hollow is more than capable of completing the task. Fox's martial arts training is going to come in handy with the way he handles the Staff, as well as how he evades attacks. He may not have the firepower he's used to, but he is still as deadly.

The most commonly used attack is the simple Staff swing. Press the Ⓐ Button to draw the Staff and to square off with an enemy. Use the ⬤ to move in close, and press the Ⓐ Button to swing the Staff.

Depending on his position relative to the enemy, Fox can be made to perform specific Staff swings by pressing the ⚪ Up, Left, or Right. Pushing the ⚪ to either side will often result in a sideways swing of the Staff (great for attacking the enemy's legs), whereas pushing Up on the ⚪ while pressing the Ⓐ Button will cause Fox to perform an overhead strike.

Fox doesn't need to fight if he doesn't want to. Although Fox will automatically face off with any bad guy he sees when the Staff is drawn, the confrontation can be avoided by pressing the ⚪ Button to put away the Staff. This is also useful for times when Fox is surrounded by multiple enemies and you prefer that he fight one of the others.

COMBINATION ATTACKS

Many of the SharpClaw in General Scales' army will only suffer damage if hit repeatedly by a combination attack. A combination attack can be initiated at any time by repeatedly pressing the Ⓐ Button. Not only do these attacks show off Fox's more stylized moves, but they often leave their target crumpled up on the ground. Whether or not the combo is successful often comes down to the fourth hit. Should the enemy manage to deflect or block the fourth strike, no damage will be delivered. This is especially true for those SharpClaw with shields and body armor.

As was the case with the standard attack, the ⚪ can be used in conjunction with the Ⓐ Button to perform modified combination attacks. The most deadly of these is Fox's Staff twirl! This attack is begun just like any other combination, but begin pulling Down on the ⚪ during Fox's third strike. He will then proceed to twirl the Staff in a whirlwind on either side of him while hitting the enemy over and over. Continue pressing the Ⓐ Button while holding Down on the ⚪ to have Fox charge the Staff with a magical energy and then smash it over his enemy's head. This last attack can break through virtually any defense.

STAFF POWERS

Although the Staff is a very capable weapon when used in its native state, it becomes truly devastating once upgraded. Throughout his adventure, Fox will encounter several upgrades for the Staff that enhance its powers considerably.

THE MIGHTY Y BUTTON

In order to quickly use any of the following Staff powers in battle, they must be assigned to the (Y) Button ahead of time. They can also be accessed from the Staff Power menu, but assigning them to the (Y) Button is easier.

FIRE BLASTER

The Fire Blaster can be used effectively in battle in two different manners, depending on the strength of the enemy. To do away with weaker enemies quickly, press the (Y) Button to draw the Fire Blaster before getting too close and press the (A) Button rapidly to destroy them before they know what hit them.

Using the Fire Blaster in this style is not recommended for larger, armor-clad enemies. Instead, begin attacking with the Staff as normal and mix in the occasionally blast from the Fire Blaster should the baddie deflect most of Fox's strikes. Defeating larger enemies is best done with combination attacks, but the Fire Blaster can help open them up for a successful combo.

ICE BLAST

Once equipped with the Ice Blast, Fox has the power to destroy any enemy both quickly and painlessly. This "freeze-n-slash" attack is performed by pressing the (Y) Button to freeze the enemy in a block of ice. Once the opponent is immobilized, press the (B) Button to switch back to normal attack mode and press Up on the (○) while pressing the (A) Button to perform an overhead strike. Any

attack will work, but we've found this to work best. Fox will bring the Staff down over the enemy's head, shattering both the ice and the baddie within.

13

GROUND QUAKE

The Ground Quake and its upgraded form, the Super Ground Quake, unleash a powerful shockwave that spreads throughout the area, knocking nearby enemies to the ground. Although this attack does render Fox's enemies defenseless for a few moments, it's typically not long enough for Fox to mount much of a follow-up attack. On the other hand, using this Staff power in combat is absolutely essential when squaring off against the crater creatures in Moon Mountain Pass and the RedEye Tribe at Walled City (requires Super Ground Quake).

EVASIVE MANEUVERS

We're not going to go so far as to say that the best offense for Fox is a great defense, but knowing when to defend, side roll, and backflip does occasionally factor into Fox's survival—especially when he's less powerful. Fox essentially has three different defensive/evasive maneuvers. For starters, Fox can be made to take a "guard" stance by pressing the ✎ Button. Fox will hold the Staff to deflect enemy attacks while taking a wide stance so as to not be pushed around too easily. Fox can block most any attack thrown at him with this move.

Another use of the ✎ Button is to shower Fox in a protective force field that will protect him from any enemy or environmental danger. In order to use this defense during combat, however, Fox must put away the Staff. Press the ● Button to put the Staff away and then hold down the ✎ Button to have him quickly put the Staff to use as a source of power for the force field.

Whereas the above two options are essentially protective measures, this final technique can be used to open up holes in the enemy's defense. By pressing the ⊠ Button during combat, Fox can be made to perform an evasive maneuver. Push Left, Right, or Down on the ◯ while pressing the ⊠ Button to have Fox roll to the left, right, or backwards, respectively. These moves are great to use when the enemy is consistently blocking Fox's attacks. Oftentimes, a roll to the side, followed by a side attack of a blast from the Fire Blaster, will be all it takes to rattle off a four-strike combination!

Another technique is to attack while coming out of a roll. If you roll left or right and immediately hit the Ⓐ Button during the roll, Fox will do a sweep kick that inflicts massive damage to the enemy. If you attack while rolling forward, Fo will perform a jump attack as well. Use these attacks to change the pace of your attacks and catch the enemy off guard.

SIDEKICK COMMANDS

Fox may touch down on Dinosaur Planet alone, but it won't take long before he has a Sidekick following his every move. Prince Tricky of the EarthWalker Tribe will be with Fox for the dino's share of this journey, and he has some very valuable skills that he just can't wait to use!

THE BASICS

When Fox first rescues Tricky from the clutches of the SharpClaw, Tricky explains to him that his father has taught him two commands: "Stay" and "Find Secret". In order to perform these skills, Tricky must be kept well fed. Fox will need to keep a stash of Blue GrubTubs on hand to give to Tricky so his energy levels don't drop too low. Once Tricky gets low on energy, he'll refuse to perform any of the commands that Fox gives him.

Tricky's initial three commands are what you'd come to expect from a dinosaur that can talk and play fetch. Give Tricky his "Stay" command (symbolized by the white hand) to make him sit down and wait for Fox to return. This command is very useful for having Tricky sit atop buttons and panels that control nearby gates. A command that's found shortly after meeting Tricky is the "Heel" command. Fox can whistle for Tricky ala the "Heel" (symbolized by a whistle) command to have him run and catch up.

The "Find Secret" command takes advantage of Tricky's superior digging ability. Give Tricky this command (symbolized by a map) whenever you encounter a dried patch of dirt or near a crack in a wall made up of dirt or snow. Unlike the previous two commands, "Find Secret" requires a bit more energy from the little Prince, so Fox will have to make sure to keep him fed if he expects to have Tricky dig up any treasure for him.

15

DO YOU HEAR SOMETHING, BOY?

Contrary to Fox's initial impressions, Tricky is wise beyond his years and can sense enemies, hidden tunnels, and buried loot well before Fox can. Pay attention to the warning signs that appear above Tricky's head as they can help Fox prepare for an upcoming battle or look closer at the ground he's traversing. An "!" will appear over Tricky's head when a bad guy is coming near. Tricky's other warning is a "?" which appears whenever a secret is nearby. Whenever the "?" appears, look closely at the immediate area and give Tricky either the "Find Secret" or "Flame" command; whichever one fits the situation.

FLAME

Eventually Tricky learns that he has the power to breathe fire and becomes ever more useful. By giving the boy his "Flame" command, Fox can have Tricky melt ice walls, light fires, burn briars, and even attack enemies. The "Flame" command is by far the most versatile of Tricky's various abilities, but it does come with a price. Not only will Tricky go through GrubTubs faster than ever before, but the flames pose a threat to Fox. Be sure to have Fox stand clear of the flames whenever Tricky is about to burn something, or else he will suffer a minimum of two blocks of damage.

ITEMS AND POWER-UPS

Fox will have the opportunity to use many items to the test during his journey around Dinosaur Planet. Although some items are merely snacks that restore lost energy, others are elaborate high-tech devices that Slippy made just for this occasion. Nearly every item can be purchased at the ThornTail Store, but the Staff upgrades can only be acquired via the underground power-up locations that exist throughout the planet.

ITEMS

DUMBLEDANG POD

These tasty treats can be found growing in trees as well as in many of the SharpClaw Crates left lying around the planet. DumbleDang Pods restore one block of energy to Fox.

You have collected a DUMBLEDANG POD.

PUKPUK EGG

PukPuk Eggs are the rare delicacy on Dinosaur Planet and it doesn't take long for Fox to develop a liking to them. Fox's best bets for finding PukPuk Eggs are inside SharpClaw Crates or at the ThornTail Store. Nevertheless, Tricky may occasionally dig one up, or a SharpClaw may even drop one after being defeated. PukPuk Eggs restore four blocks of energy to Fox.

BAFOMDAD

Not much is known about these magical creatures other than their mystical ability to allow Fox to continue his journey even after losing the last of his energy. Fox can only carry one BafomDad without a proper BafomDad Holder.

BafomDad Holder

This special satchel allows Fox to carry up to ten BafomDads at once. Be sure to purchase it from the ThornTail Store as soon as Fox can afford it.

Bomb Spore

When planted in a Bomb Spore Planting Patch, a Bomb Spore will swiftly grow into a Bomb Spore Plant. All Fox has to do is shoot one with the Fire Blaster to see where they get their name from. Bomb Spores can be acquired by shooting a mature Bomb Spore Plant (not one that Fox planted). Fox can carry a maximum of seven Bomb Spores.

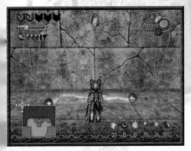

Fuel Cell

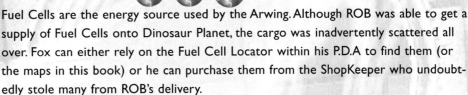

Fuel Cells are the energy source used by the Arwing. Although ROB was able to get a supply of Fuel Cells onto Dinosaur Planet, the cargo was inadvertently scattered all over. Fox can either rely on the Fuel Cell Locator within his P.D.A to find them (or the maps in this book) or he can purchase them from the ShopKeeper who undoubtedly stole many from ROB's delivery.

Blue GrubTub Fungus

These wily little mushrooms are Tricky's favorite snack, but unfortunately prove too evasive for the little dinosaur to catch. Fox will need to thwack them with the Staff to stun them and then grab hold of them for when Tricky gets hungry. Fox can carry a maximum of 15 GrubTubs at once.

FireFly

FireFlies are invaluable to Fox when he enters dark places such as the ancient well in ThornTail Hollow. Fox must have the FireFly Lantern in order to carry any FireFlies. FireFlies can often be found near the darkest areas of Dinosaur Planet and can be used to illuminate Fox's path for nearly a full minute!

FireFly Lantern

Fox will need to purchase this item before the ThornTail in the ancient well lets him descend to the caves below. This item can be used for storing up to 31 FireFlies, but only one can be used at a time.

Rock Candy

This sugary snack may not seem edible to you or I, but to a WarpStone, nothing can be sweeter. Sometimes you have to give a little to get something big in return. Try giving the cranky old WarpStone a gift he can't refuse.

Hi-Def Display

Slippy made these zoom goggles especially for Fox's trip to Dinosaur Planet, but that no good ShopKeeper got ahold of them before Fox did. When equipped, press the ⬤ Button to switch to first-person view and use the Ⓒ to zoom in and out. These fancy goggles even have a built-in compass. Way to go Slippy!

DINOSAUR HORN

This is the DINOSAUR HORN

This sacred instrument will allow Fox to summon a SnowHorn for trips through bad storms. It will also be used to prove to the SnowHorn that Fox is worthy of entering the Krazoa Shrine deep within their land.

TRICKY'S BALL

As much as Fox might wish otherwise, Tricky is just a young boy and needs to be played with from time to time. Spend some time tossing the ol' ball around with Tricky and he might just surprise you one day.

CHEAT TOKEN

Not much is known about these magical coins. Perhaps they can be used to make a wish?

SNOWHORN ARTIFACT

This pricy item was the prized possession of the SnowHorn near the lake in SnowHorn Wastes. If only he could make the trip to ThornTail Hollow and buy it back...

STAFF UPGRADES

Fox will have to keep his eyes peeled for underground power-up locations if he's to ever acquire all of these enhancements, but it's worth it! Fox will need each and every one of these abilities if he's to ever reunite Dinosaur Planet.

FIRE BLASTER

The Fire Blaster is used in battle as well as an important tool in exploration. Many orange panels that are seen throughout the lands need to be hit with a blast from the Fire Blaster in order to open a nearby gate or entranceway. The Fire Blaster is found in a cave in ThornTail Hollow. (See the *ThornTail Hollow* chapter of the walkthrough.)

ROCKET BOOST

Together with an activated Rocket Boost Pad, the Rocket Boost enhancement allows Fox to soar into the air onto ledges that are otherwise unreachable. Press and hold the Ⓐ Button to use. (See the *SpellStone #1* chapter of the walkthrough.)

18

ICE BLAST

The Ice Blast is capable of freezing enemies in a temporary block of ice (which can be smashed into pieces), as well as for dousing flames. Like the Fire Blaster, this upgrade is well-used both in combat and exploration. (See the *SpellStone #1* chapter of the walkthrough.)

GROUND QUAKE

The Ground Quake is primarily used for stunning enemies that would otherwise be immune to Fox's attacks. In particular, the Ground Quake is used almost exclusively to battle the crater creatures of Moon Mountain Pass. Fox will also utilize this upgrade's strength when trying to trigger certain events in the Walled City. (See the *Moon Pass Mountain* chapter of the walkthrough.)

PORTAL DEVICE

This enhancement is strictly for exploratory purposes and serves no function in battle. With the Portal Device, Fox will be able to unlock the enormous stone seals that block the path in certain areas of Dinosaur Planet. (See the *SpellStone #3* chapter of the walkthrough.)

SUPER GROUND QUAKE

This is essentially a bigger and better version of the Ground Quake and is needed strictly when dealing with members of the RedEye Tribe. (See the *SpellStone #3* chapter of the walkthrough.)

THORNTAIL STORE

Fox may be going it alone in this journey across Dinosaur Planet, but he won't ever be too far from a reliable supply store. The proprietor of the ThornTail Store may not offer the most personalized service, and he can be downright rude at times, but his selection is top notch nonetheless. There's something to fit every budget so be sure to stop by whenever passing through the Hollow, no matter how few Scarabs you have.

DINOSAUR CURRENCY

The currency of choice on Dinosaur Planet is the Scarab, a small glowing insect that lives in casks and under rocks. Scarabs come in three different denominations: 1 (green), 5 (red), and 10 (gold) and can be used (1) for purchasing items at the ThornTail Store, paying the toll to Cape Claw and (2) for bribing the occasional BribeClaw.

The ShopKeeper may not be the friendliest face in ThornTail Hollow, but he is at least willing to negotiate a good deal. When Fox selects an item he's considering purchasing, the ShopKeeper will slither over and hold up a sign that shows his asking price. Use the ⊙ to lower the price and press the Ⓐ Button to see if he'll take the offer. The ShopKeeper will then let Fox know if the price is acceptable or too low. Although Scarabs are always just a stone's toss away, literally, it's certainly fun to haggle. Just keep in mind, however, that the ShopKeeper will toss Fox out of his store if Fox makes three consecutive offers that are too low.

How to Haggle

The ShopKeeper will consider some counter-offers, but he's not always going to accept any offer that's too far from his original asking price. Suggest a price that's roughly 20% less than the asking price and see what he says. If the ShopKeeper refuses this price, make a second offer that's 10% less than the asking original asking price. If this offer gets refused, just go ahead and pay his normal asking price. The ShopKeeper will occasionally accept a lower price for an item, but it all depends on his mood. Don't expect him to accept the same offer every day.

The ThornTail Store contains three rooms of wares: supplies, special goods, and maps. In addition, there is a little alcove tucked away in each of the middle and right-hand rooms that contain extra items, as well as a Rocket Boost Pad that can propel Fox up to the balcony above. There, he will be able to break open several casks to find some of the ShopKeeper's Scarabs.

ThornTail Store Goods

ITEM	ASKING PRICE	COUNTER-OFFER
DumbleDang Pod	3	2
SnowHorn Wastes Map	5	4
Walled City Map	5	4
CloudRunner Fortress Map	5	4
DarkIce Mines	5	4
LightFoot Village Map	5	4
Moon Pass Map	5	4
ThornTail Hollow Map	5	4
Cape Claw Map	5	4
Bomb Spore	5	4
Krazoa Palace Map	5	4
Dragon Rock Map	5	4
PukPuk Egg	6	4
Fuel Cell	10	7
Ocean Force Point Map	10	7
Volcano Force Point Map	10	7
DumbleDang Pods	10	7
FireFly	10	7

ThornTail Store Goods Continued

ITEM	ASKING PRICE	COUNTER-OFFER
Rock Candy	10	7
GrubTub Fungus	12	10
Tricky's Ball	15	12
PukPuk Eggs	15	12
Cheat Token	20	16
Hi-Def Display Device	20	16
FireFly Lantern	20	16
BafomDad Holder	20	16
SnowHorn Artifact	130	120

THE SCARAB ROOM

In addition to the various rooms of goods, the ThornTail Store also contains the entertaining Scarab Room—yesssss! Head down either of the ramps flanking the exit and talk to the ShopKeeper. Here Fox can place bets over how many Scarabs he can chase down in thirty seconds. The ShopKeeper will then throw that number of Scarabs into the cave and it back and watch as Fox tries to collect them all.

Although Fox gets to keep the Scarabs if he collects the amount he wagered, he must also cough up that same number of Scarabs if he fails. As if collecting a bunch of fleeing insects wasn't tough enough, the ShopKeeper makes things more difficult by releasing several black Scarabs as well. Fox must avoid these Scarabs as they deduct one Scarab from the total collected and will certainly cause Fox to lose his bet.

PILOTING THE ARWING

Fox McCloud must pilot the Arwing to the floating worlds in order to retrieve the SpellStones. With help from his friends, Slippy and Peppy, Fox will need to navigate through various obstacles and reach these worlds intact. Each of these four floating worlds is protected by a Force Field. Flying through various numbers of Gold Rings will lower the Force Field and enable Fox to land safely.

As your quest progresses the Arwing Missions will get tougher and require more Gold Rings, so learn the controls and keep an eye on the Arwing's energy.

CONTROLS

Control	Action
Up on (stick)	Dive
Down on (stick)	Climb
Left on (stick)	Bank Left
Right on (stick)	Bank Right
A Button	Fires the Lasers
B Button	Fires a Bomb, must first pick up a Bomb upgrade
L Button	Hold to bank Left tightly, press once for barrel roll
R Button	Hold to bank Right tightly, press once for barrel roll
X Button	Air Break—Reduce speed
Y Button	Booster—Burst of speed
(C) Button	Communicator

POINT VALUES

As the Arwing flies through the rings or destroys the mines, ships and asteroids, points will be given as follows:

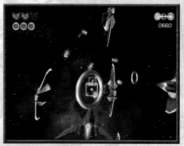

OBJECT	POINTS
Supply Ring (Silver Ring)	10

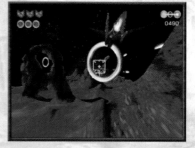

OBJECT	POINTS
Gold Ring	20

OBJECT	POINTS
X inside Gold Ring	15

OBJECT	POINTS
S Upgrade Box	15

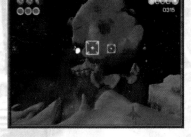

OBJECT	POINTS
Smart Bomb/Laser Upgrade	25

OBJECT	POINTS
Asteroid	5

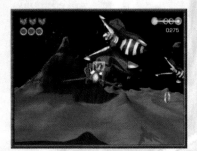

OBJECT	POINTS
Mine	10

OBJECT	POINTS
Enemy Ship	20

TIPS

Use the ⬒ Button and ⬒ Button to reach the Gold Rings easier. An extra spin towards a ring can make the difference in getting that last required Gold Ring.

Flying through a Silver Ring will restore one block of the Arwing's energy as well as give a point bonus.

Special Crates are marked with an "S" and can be shot and picked up to give the Arwing a Laser upgrade or Bomb upgrade.

Use the Bombs wisely, wait for a group of enemy ships or mines. The more you take out with the Bomb, the better the score.

At times a Gold Ring will be blocked by an X. Shoot out the X before reaching the Gold Ring in order to get credit for the Ring.

After each mission, your score will be ranked with previous attempts at that mission. Try the missions again later to better your score.

THE ARWING MISSIONS

Fox will fly the Arwing up to the Four Floating Worlds and back to Dinosaur Planet for five different Arwing Missions.

FUEL CONSUMPTION

Collect Fuel Cells left by ROB on the surface of Dinosaur Planet to power the Arwing. The Arwing will consume more fuel in the later Arwing flights.

LOCATION	FUEL CELLS REQUIRED
Dinosaur Planet	0
DarkIce Mines	5
CloudRunner Fortress	10
Walled City	12
Dragon Rock	15

24

GOLD RINGS REQUIRED

In order to travel to and from the four floating worlds, the Arwing must travel through a set number of rings to lower the Force Field. Even after going through the required number of rings, the Arwing must still reach the end safely.

Fly through 3 Gold Rings to open the Force Field.

LOCATION	GOLD RINGS
Dinosaur Planet	1
DarkIce Mines	3
CloudRunner Fortress	5
Walled City	7
Dragon Rock	10

Up in Space

Detailed tips on finding each and every required Gold Ring can be found in the *SpellStone* chapters throughout the walkthrough.

A MERCENARY'S GUIDE TO DINOSAUR PLANET

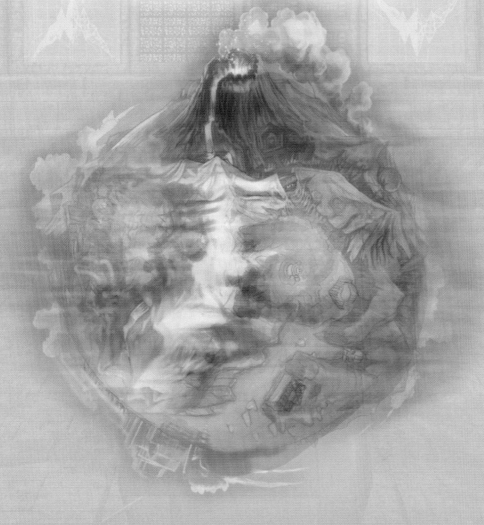

PROLOGUE: A DISTRESS CALL IS ANSWERED

Orphaned and cast astray after her home planet was inexplicably destroyed, Krystal finds herself scouring the Lylat System in a hunt for answers. Finally, after searching for thousands of miles, Krystal receives a muddled distress signal from a little-known part of the galaxy known as Dinosaur Planet. The signaler's concerns were unclear, but she sensed urgency in the message and decides to brave the fierce storm to investigate.

Just as Krystal and her CloudRunner friend begin the descent to the planet below, several large fireballs come scorching by. Before evasive maneuvers can be made, one of the fireballs hits home and knocks Krystal's magical Staff from her grip. There's no time to think about the loss, however, as a well-armed, flying galleon suddenly overtakes the pair. Its intentions are clear—Krystal is in a fight for her life!

RUMBLE IN THE NIGHT SKY

NOTE | INVINCIBILITY

Worried that you haven't had time to learn the controls? Don't sweat it, for as big and bad as the galleon seems, Krystal will not suffer damage during this sequence.

Krystal may have lost her Staff, but the CloudRunner is not nearly as defenseless. The game begins once the pairing pulls into position behind the galleon. Use the ○ to steer the pair and press the Ⓐ Button to attack. During the first phase of the battle, focus attacks on the dragonhead statues from which the fireballs are launched. Once the dragonheads have each been hit four times, they will catch fire and the second phase of the battle ensues.

The mysterious captain of the ship decides to put the propeller to use against Krystal. Attack the tips of the propeller blades to break them off one at a time as the ship backs into the pairing. Try to evade the blades as best as possible, but take solace in the fact that Krystal and her friend will not be harmed even if hit.

Once the prop is fully disabled, the third phase of this battle will begin. The flames on the dragonhead statues have been extinguished and the fireballs are back! Launch an all-out offensive on the statues to polish them off for good. As was the case in the first phase of this fight, each statue needs to be hit four times in order to destroy it.

Just because the ship is without its propeller and rear fireballs, doesn't mean that the fight is over. Although it may seem that the galleon is retreating, it's actually just turning around to face Krystal head on. The galleon's most prominent feature is a fireball-spitting dinosaur head mounted to the bow of the ship—and here it comes! Dodge the fireballs and land four attacks on the head of the dinosaur to defeat the ship once and for all.

SEARCHING THE GALLEON

NOTE   FOXY LADY

Krystal becomes susceptible to damage once she sets foot on the ship. Take care of the lass, as her fate is linked to that of powerful events that are, for now, beyond comprehension.

Krystal will set the CloudRunner down on the rear of the ship and send him on his way, for she is prepared to go it alone from here on in. Descend the steps and cross the deck towards the bow. Climb the stairs at the front of the ship and approach the birdcage to be given instructions on using the all-purpose Ⓐ Button . Press the Ⓐ Button to talk to the caged bird. Doing so will open a pair of doors at the rear of the ship.

Leave the bird and descend through the newly opened doors to the cabins below. There, on a pedestal in the center of the room, lies the **Krazoa Palace Key**. Approach the key and press the Ⓐ Button to pick it up. Head back up the stairs and approach the birdcage once again.

This time the bird isn't doing much talking. Instead, General Scales, the fierce ruler of Dinosaur Planet, bursts through a nearby door and begins threatening Krystal. Her pleas fall on deaf ears and the brute hastily grabs her by the neck and tosses her petite body overboard. Fortunately, the CloudRunner overheard the commotion and swoops in to save Krystal from certain death. General Scales' tirade concerning Dinosaur Planet only served to make Krystal that much more determined to follow the distress signal.

You dare to challenge me?

KRAZOA PALACE PART 1

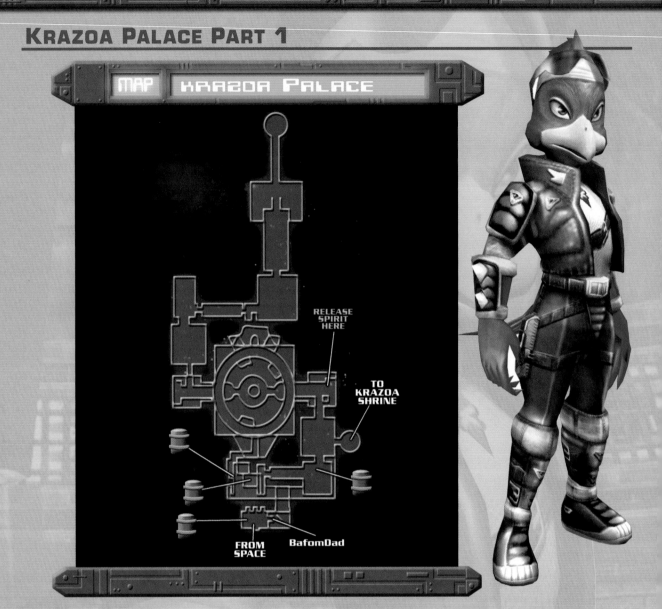

MAP KRAZOA PALACE

RELEASE SPIRIT HERE

TO KRAZOA SHRINE

FROM SPACE

BafomDad

The CloudRunner will follow the cries for help to Krazoa Palace, the most sacred place in Dinosaur Planet. Say farewell to the CloudRunner and approach the weary EarthWalker near the locked doors. He will tell of the dangers at the Palace and how to use the Ⓧ Button to roll out of harm's way. Let him tend to his guard duty and approach the door on the far left. Use Ⓒ to select the Krazoa Palace Key from the inventory and unlock the door with it. Inside, Krystal will find a Fuel Barrel. Press the Ⓐ Button to shoulder the Barrel and head back outside into the rain. Krystal can use these explosives to break open SharpClaw Crates and to destroy enemies.

PLAYING KEEP AWAY   TIP

The glowing squid-like creatures seen hovering about the Palace can be destroyed with a well-tossed Fuel Barrel, but since they respawn after several seconds, it's best to just let them be. Try to give them a wide berth or use the Ⓧ Button to roll past them if they come too close.

Toss the Fuel Barrel at the crate directly across from the room to discover a **DumbleDang Pod**. This tasty fruit can restore two blocks of energy. Other crates contain **PukPuk Eggs**, which restore one full badge of energy (four blocks).

Now that Krystal has used a Fuel Barrel, the metal Fuel Barrel Generator in the center of the platform will function properly. These circular plates are a reliable source of Fuel Barrels, however a new one will not appear until the previous one is detonated. Grab another Fuel Barrel and use it destroy the crates blocking the ramp leading down towards the Palace entrance.

Take a second Fuel Barrel down the ramp and enter the room to the left. Toss the Fuel Barrel at the large crack in the wall to blow a hole in the wall. Talk to the two other EarthWalkers to gain further instructions on using the controls. Krystal can break open the small casks outside by throwing them to the ground. These casks each contain a **PukPuk Egg**.

Meet up with the EarthWalker trapped inside the Palace and use the Fuel Barrel behind him to demolish the crates blocking the entryway to the next room. Don't head down that hall just yet! Venture further down the main hallway and equip Krystal with another Fuel Barrel first.

NOTE — KRAZOA SPIRITS

As suspected, General Scales (with his unquenchable greed) was the reason a distress call was sent out. The EarthWalkers were sent by their King to defend the Palace and to protect the six sacred Krazoa Spirits from the General and his army. As the SharpClaw army battled their way past the EarthWalker defenses, a decision was made to hide the Krazoa Spirits throughout the planet. Krazoa Palace must be made safe for the return of the Spirits if the dinosaur tribes are to ever live in peace again.

The corridor near the trapped EarthWalker is booby-trapped with three flame-throwing jets. There are roughly 4 seconds between each flame burst when it is safe for Krystal to sneak by unharmed. Carefully navigate the flaming corridor and toss the Fuel Barrel at the cracked wall at the opposite end to gain entrance to the more lavish part of the Palace.

Take the Fuel Barrel and approach the shrine at the front of the room. The black panel in the floor is linked to the large doors near the sunlight and must be kept depressed so Krystal can proceed. Press the Ⓐ Button while standing on the panel to place the Fuel Barrel down. The Fuel Barrel is heavy enough to hold the doors open while Krystal enters the next room.

Approach the exhausted EarthWalker in the next room and listen to his lesson on the Krazoa Spirits. In order for Dinosaur Planet to remain a healthy and peaceful place, someone pure of heart must take the Krazoa Tests. Those who complete the tests will be given the opportunity to return a Krazoa Spirit to the Palace. Step on the Krazoa Shrine Entrance Warp in the room the EarthWalker reveals to attempt the first Krazoa Test.

NOTE | About the Shrines

The Krazoa Shrines are separate from the Palace and can only be reached through the Entrance Warps. Once at a Shrine, the player must navigate a brief series of obstacle-laden rooms to locate the hidden Krazoa Spirit. Succeed at its test and the Krazoa Spirit will be yours to deliver back to the Krazoa Palace.

KRAZOA TEST

1 Climb the ladder in the corner alcove to enter the first corridor. Dodge the flames and the floating creature and approach the Life-Force Door. Grab the Fuel Barrel and throw it at the enemy in the pit to satisfy the Spirit requirement of the Life-Force Door.

2 Enter the next hallway and stand on the black panel to raise the gate at the far end. Make a quick study of the three flame jets and dash past them towards the gate as it closes. Press the Ⓧ Button to somersault under the gate if it's going to be a close call.

The glowing transparent mask in the center of the next room is the first of six Krazoa Spirits. This Spirit will test your observational skills by hiding in one of six shuffling urns. The test is to see if you can identify which urn the Spirit has hidden in. Choose correctly three times in a row and the Spirit will surrender itself as a reward.

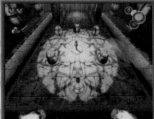

The urns move at random so we cannot identify which of them the Spirit will be in during each trial. Nevertheless, the urns move slowly enough that they can be followed without too much difficulty. As an aid, we suggest either tracing the correct urn's path with your finger on the television screen (be careful not to smudge the glass) or by using the Ⓞ to guide Krystal around the room in a similar fashion. Once the urns stop moving, run up to the one with the Spirit in it to make your choice. If correct, the Spirit will continue the test. If the choice was wrong, Krystal will be instantly warped back to the entrance of the Shrine.

The Life-Force Doors can only be entered when a number of enemies, equal to the number of Spirits in the Door, are destroyed. The monsters needing to be defeated are not always near the Life-Force Door so don't get discouraged, just keep looking around.

KRAZOA PALACE PART 2

After completing the Test of Observation, Krystal will be warped back to the Palace. Return to the EarthWalker in the adjacent room and listen to his reasons for his releasing the Spirit: only when the Spirits are freed in Krazoa Palace will they possibly be able to stop the war between the dinosaur tribes and the SharpClaw.

Step onto the golden pedestal emblazoned with an image depicting the alignment of the six Krazoa Spirits. This platform will rise up, allowing Krystal to reach the tunnel in the wall. Turn to the right at the end of this tunnel and approach the Krazoa statue mounted on the wall. Press the (A) Button to release the Spirit from within.

As the Spirit is released and the Spirit Collector harnesses its power, someone—or something—appears from the shadows and tosses Krystal into the beam of energy. The beam delivers the would-be heroine to a large crystal, inside which she becomes trapped.

Krystal's journey has come to an impromptu end. Unless, of course, an adventurous rescuer should happen by this corner of the Lylat System…in need of a fox to call his own.

THORNTAIL HOLLOW

As it turns out, Krystal wasn't the only one to receive that distress call. A group of experienced mercenaries known as the Star Fox team was informed of the crisis by their commander, General Pepper. The General informed the team that the ancient world of Dinosaur Planet was being torn apart from an unidentifiable force and it was up to them to piece the planet back together again. Unfortunately, the only lead General Pepper was able to provide was that the Queen of the EarthWalker tribe may be able to help. The Star Fox team, led by experienced pilot Fox McCloud, has been adrift in the Lylat System for years and welcomes every opportunity to make some extra cash. Naturally, the team accepts the missions.

Slippy! It's General Pepper!

Set course for Dinosaur Planet!

NOTE | SPACE FLIGHTS

The Star Fox team's primary ship is far too large to set down on Dinosaur Planet, so Fox must travel alone in his trusty Arwing space cruiser. Select "Dinosaur Planet" from the large, 3D space map. Fox will return to this screen whenever he needs to fly to one of the outlying worlds.

SPACE TRAVEL

DESTINATION: THORNTAIL HOLLOW

Fuel Cells Needed: N/A

Gold Rings: 1 of 10

Time: 1:00

Although the Arwing has been pre-fueled for this trip, Fox will need to retrieve the Fuel Cells that ROB drops for him on Dinosaur Planet in order to make future flights. Even then, space travel isn't just about topping off the tank. Fox will need to fly through a set number of Gold Rings in order to open the Force Field that shields each location. Be sure to read "Piloting the Arwing" in the *Mission Basics* chapter of this book for more information.

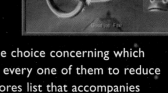
Good job, Fox!

The Force Field on Dinosaur Planet can be opened by flying through just 1 Gold Ring and is, therefore, the least complicated shell to crack. Any of the 10 Gold Rings can be flown through in order to open the Force Field, so the choice concerning which one is up to you. We recommend trying to pilot the craft through each and every one of them to reduce the chance of failure—and for the practice! As an added bonus, the High Scores list that accompanies each trip provides special recognition to those who navigate through all 10 Gold Rings.

SPACE TRAVEL cont.

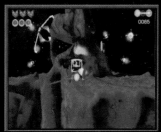

From the start of the flight, stick to the center of the screen and continue blasting away with the Arwing's laser cannons. While passing the first large island, make sure to avoid (or shoot down) the three approaching enemy ships. Dodge the two asteroids and then aim the ship at the lower hole in the rock tower on the second island. In the center of the hole awaits the first Gold Ring. Grab this one, as many of the other Rings require more cockpit finesse to obtain.

Although the Force Field may be opened as soon as the Arwing flies through a Gold Ring, Fox must still pilot the ship out of the asteroid belt in order to reach the destination. Spend the remaining time blasting away at the asteroids, mines, and enemy ships so as to score additional points and, more importantly, to reduce the odds of crashing into something. Although most bumps and scrapes will only inflict one block of damage to the ship, a head-on crash with a large asteroid or island will cause the ship to explode. Steer the Arwing through Silver Rings to regain one block of lost energy. Lastly, be

sure to blast open the Special Crates and grab either the Laser Upgrade or Bomb Upgrade power-ups that appear. They can help clear a path through all but the most congested of areas.

FINDING QUEEN EARTHWALKER PART 1

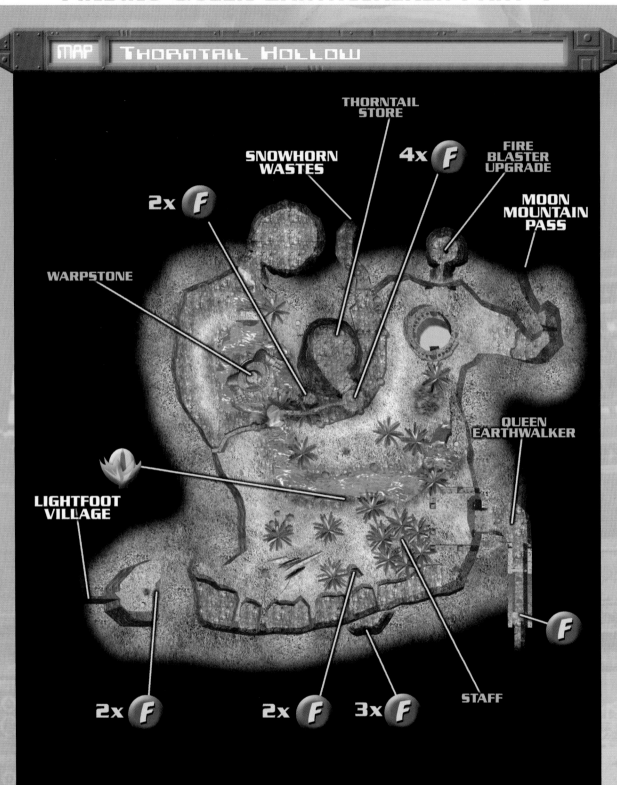

MAP THORNTAIL HOLLOW

THORNTAIL STORE

SNOWHORN WASTES

4x **F**

FIRE BLASTER UPGRADE

MOON MOUNTAIN PASS

2x **F**

WARPSTONE

QUEEN EARTHWALKER

LIGHTFOOT VILLAGE

2x **F**   2x **F**   3x **F**

STAFF

F

Fox will set the Arwing down in a lush corner of Dinosaur Planet named ThornTail Hollow. This area is a relative safe-haven and will serve as a hub for Fox throughout the game. In addition to being a great place to leave the Arwing unattended, the Hollow is home to the ThornTail Store, a perfect stop to stock up on supplies!

The first thing Fox should do after arriving in this world is talk to the ThornTail standing near the nose of the Arwing. ThornTails, for the most part, are very intelligent and helpful creatures and should be spoken with at every opportunity. This one explains that Queen EarthWalker has been locked behind the doors of a nearby temple. General Pepper was right; these guys are a big help!

Since this mission will undoubtedly involve kicking some SharpClaw tail, Fox had better arm himself. As luck would have it, Krystal was directly above the Hollow when the fireball knocked the staff from her grasp. The **Staff** can be found sticking out of the ground amongst the nearby field of flowers. Fox will receive a brief telepathic message from Krystal describing his find. The Staff is not just a weapon to be used in combat, but can eventually be relied upon in a host of different situations.

FOX'S FIRST BATTLE

Continue past the flowers towards the temple set against the cliffs. Just as Fox enters the squared courtyard in front of the temple, four SharpClaw will come out and attack. Press the (A) Button to draw the Staff and to face off with one of the assailants. These particular SharpClaw have just a spiked club and light armor to defend themselves with.

Repeatedly press the (A) Button to initiate a combo attack against the chosen enemy. It will take four successive hits to inflict two blocks of damage to him. After taking damage, the SharpClaw will momentarily lie on the ground stunned and motionless. Initiate a follow-up combo at this time to finish him off.

NOTE   FIGHT FAIR!

As rude and crude as the SharpClaw seem, you have to give them credit for fighting fair! Despite having a numbers advantage in nearly every encounter, the SharpClaw will take turns fighting Fox one-on-one. Fox will square off with whichever SharpClaw is standing in front of him when he draws the Staff. To fight a different attacker, quickly press the (B) Button to put away the staff, turn to face another enemy, and tap the (A) Button to draw the weapon once again.

Whereas the first SharpClaw may have fallen easily, many in General Scales' army know how to use their weapons and armor to block Fox's attacks. To get around this, try using the ⊙ in conjunction with the Ⓐ Button when attacking. Pushing in different directions with the ⊙ will cause Fox to focus his attacks low, high, or to the various sides of the enemy. Using the ⊙ during combination attacks is especially valuable.

Another strategy that often works is to assume a defensive posture and allow your opponent to take the first swipe. Press the ⟲ Button to defend against its attack and then immediately counter with the Staff. Similarly, Fox can be made to dodge attacks by using the ⊙ together with the Ⓧ Button. For more detailed explanations of Fox's unique combat abilities, be sure to read 'Combat Tactics' in the *Mission Basics* chapter.

FINDING QUEEN EARTHWALKER PART 2

Once the last of the four SharpClaw are defeated, a red panel will appear high above the temple doors and a second message from Krystal will play. By defeating the SharpClaw at the temple, Fox has proven himself worthy of becoming the new master of the Staff. Leave the courtyard and enter the cave that opened during Krystal's message.

The Staff will emit a green glow as Fox draws closer to the speckled-blue stone in the center of the cave. Press the Ⓐ Button near the stone to pry it up to reveal a hole in the ground. Drop through the hole to enter an underground room containing numerous Staff Energy Gems. Jump across the small pond to the center platform and press the Ⓐ Button to collect the first Staff upgrade: the **Fire Blaster**. The Fire Blaster enables the Staff to discharge a small fire-based charge that can be used to shoot enemies from a distance or to turn the various orange and green panels on and off.

QUICKDRAW MCCLOUD   TIP

Use the ⊙ to select the Fire Blaster upgrade from the yellow inventory panel and press the Ⓨ Button to assign it. By doing so, you will be able to have Fox quickly grab the Staff and start blasting by simply pressing the Ⓨ Button! Also, it is possible to fire off a round or two from the Fire Blaster in the middle of a battle by pressing the Ⓨ Button amidst the flurry of attacks.

Approach the gate barring the way out of the cave and use the Fire Blaster to shoot the orange panel on the rock wall. Line up the crosshairs with the panel and press the Ⓐ Button to fire. Head back up the hill and press the Ⓐ Button while standing in the sunlight to exit the area.

Now that Fox is armed with the Fire Blaster, he can return to the temple where he fought the SharpClaw and blast the panel over the doors. Be careful when rounding the area by the large circular structure, as a pair of winged creatures will attack. Fox can defend himself by swinging the Staff, but this is a great opportunity to practice using the Fire Blaster. Just keep in mind that Fox will need to gather up Energy Gems from the Magic Plants in order to keep the Staff powered-up. Swing the Staff at a Magic Plant to make it drop its Energy Gem.

The temple's enormous stone door will open once Fox hits the orange panel with the Fire Blaster. Rush inside to see if Queen EarthWalker is still alright. The Queen appreciates Fox's efforts, but is overwhelmed by the disappearance of her son, Prince Tricky. She needs Fox to search for the missing Prince in the Ice Mountain area; the WarpStone can help him with transportation.

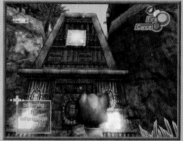 

NOTE | SAVE IT!

Star Fox Adventures features a save-anytime feature that is extremely beneficial to the player—if you remember to use it! Get in the habit of saving your progress whenever an objective is completed or when Fox has full health and Staff Energy.

A GIFT FOR THE WARPSTONE PART 1

It's easy to understand the Queen's concern over her son, but Fox can't just rush off on another errand; first he's got to do some exploration. And there's no better place to start than in the Queen's small sanctuary. Head up the ramp to find the first **Fuel Cell**.

NOTE | FUEL CELLS

ROB the Robot encountered some trouble when making the cargo drop and the Fuel Cells have gotten scattered all over the planet. Even worse, some of them ended up in the hands of the SharpClaw! Fox must collect the Fuel Cells during his explorations if he's to ever fly the Arwing off this rock. Use the ✦ to access the Fuel Cell Locator mode of the P.D.A. The blinking arrow in the locator screen will help guide you to Fuel Cells.

Exit the temple and follow the stream towards the center of the Hollow. Growing along its banks is a Bomb Spore Plant. Use the Fire Blaster to detonate it and collect the **Bomb Spores** that float down to the ground. Fox can carry up to three Bomb Spores at a time.

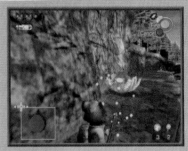

Follow the stream back towards the temple and climb onto the ledge near the cliffs on the right. Fox will encounter a Bomb Spore Planting Patch just before the first gap in the ledge. Select a Bomb Spore from the red panel of the inventory screen to plant it. Once it grows, stand back and shoot a beam from the Fire Blaster at it to blow a hole into the secret cave inside the cliff. Enter the cave and collect the three **Fuel Cells**, as well as the **Scarabs** that are inside the casks.

NOTE   CRITTER CURRENCY

The glowing insects known as Scarabs serve as the currency on Dinosaur Planet and can be used to buy various items from the ThornTail Store. Fox will also need to keep a ready supply of Scarabs on hand in order to grease a few palms during his adventure. There are three colors of Scarabs and each are worth a different value. Green Scarabs have a value of 1, red Scarabs are worth 5, and orange Scarabs are worth 10. The more valuable ones are pretty evasive, so get after them quickly or they'll disappear for good!

Exit the cave and run to the left on the top of the ledge. Fox will automatically leap when he gets to the edge, so don't worry about falling. Continue leaping across the gaps to the far end of this ledge. Insert the Staff into the slot next to the orange panel to raise the gate below. Return the way you came and leap onto the outcropping near the front of the Arwing to pick up two more **Fuel Cells**.

Jump off the ledge and approach the ThornTail near the circle of rocks by the water to learn of a surprise lurking under the stones. Press the (A) Button repeatedly while standing near the rocks to use the Staff to pry them up off the ground. The surprise the ThornTail referred to is a large stash of Scarabs hidden under each of the rocks.

CASH MACHINES   TIP

Money may not grow on trees, but Scarabs do grow under rocks! The circle of rocks in ThornTail Hollow is the single most reliable source of cash in all of Dinosaur Planet. Be sure to line Fox's pockets whenever passing through this area.

ThornTail Store

Now that Fox has some spending money, it's time to head to the ThornTail Store. Wade across the stream and enter the large doorway between the lanterns to descend into the shop. The ShopKeeper stocks many items that will aid Fox throughout his journey. The Store consists of three main shopping areas that include basic supplies, special goods, and maps. In addition, there's an area called the Scarab Room where Fox can gamble with the ShopKeeper.

NOTE Shopping Spree

The 'ThornTail Store' section of the *Mission Basics* contains a complete listing of everything the ShopKeeper sells and its corresponding price. Not only that, but you'll also find item-specific tips for haggling and pointers on how to succeed at the Scarab Game.

Since Fox can only carry a maximum of 10 Scarabs at this point in the game, he will need to return to the circle of rocks to pry up more money in order to outfit himself for the upcoming trip to Ice Mountain. Although it's never a bad idea to fill up Fox's energy meter with DumbleDang Pods and PukPuk Eggs, they are not the reason for the shopping trip. It's customary practice in the Lylat System to offer a gift to those who provide special services, as the WarpStone does. And no gift could be finer than a nice chunk of **Rock Candy** (10 Scarabs). Enter the middle room of the Store and purchase the gift for the WarpStone.

Although the Rock Candy is the only necessary purchase for now, Fox's P.D.A contains a handy map feature that comes in handy when investigating new areas. Leave the store to load up on Scarabs and then return to purchase the ThornTail Hollow Map and the SnowHorn Wastes map, both of which can be found in the right-hand room. These maps will automatically be loaded into the P.D.A whenever Fox enters an area covered on one of them. Use the ✛ to zoom in and out on the map screen.

A GIFT FOR THE WARPSTONE PART 2

Before heading to the WarpStone, drop into the stream and follow it to the base of the waterfall to find another Bomb Spore Planting Patch. Plant and detonate another Bomb Spore to reveal a hidden cave. Follow the underground tunnel to a storage room housing some SharpClaw Crates and four **Fuel Cells**.

Head back through the opening in the waterfall and climb the hill to the sleepy ThornTail by the cracked wall. Plant another Bomb Spore and use the Fire Blaster on it to blow a hole in the wall. Return to the Bomb Spore Plant near the stream to load up on more Bomb Spores and then continue up the path past the ThornTail.

Before Fox disturbs the WarpStone, he ought to plant a Bomb Spore in the Planting Patch beside the pool of water. Igniting a Bomb Spore Plant near the crack in the wall will reveal another secret cave containing a SharpClaw Crate with a DumbleDang Pod and two **Fuel Cells**.

Hop across the water onto the raised pad near the WarpStone and offer him the Rock Candy. The mighty WarpStone enjoys the gift, but is quite reluctant to help Fox at first. Fortunately, he eventually remembers his role on Dinosaur Planet and instructs Fox to select between Ice Mountain, the Game Well Maze, and Krazoa Palace. Push to the Left on the ⓞ to select Ice Mountain; the other places will have to wait!

ICE MOUNTAIN & SNOWHORN WASTES

Thanks to the WarpStone, Fox arrives at Ice Mountain just in time to see Prince Tricky get dropped off from a large spacecraft. Unfortunately, two SharpClaw brutes are there to receive the lad and immediately start bullying him. Just when it looks as if Prince Tricky is going to cry, the two hurry him into a bunker built into the mountain and seal the steel door behind them. It's up to Fox to find a way in!

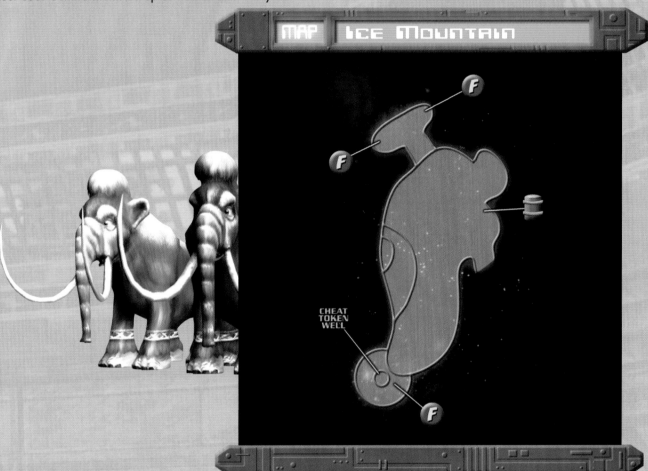

MAP — ICE MOUNTAIN

CHEAT TOKEN WELL

OPERATION: RESCUE PRINCE TRICKY

Ice Mountain is actually a very small area connected to the much more expansive SnowHorn Wastes via a series of narrow valleys. The SharpClaw value the seclusion of Ice Mountain and have turned it into a prison of sorts, even though they rely on the harsh weather and terrain as their primary defenses.

93

From Fox's entrypoint, turn to the left to find a SharpClaw Crate, a Magical Plant, and a Fuel Barrel. Grab the Fuel Barrel and carry it down the main trail to the large barricade of SharpClaw crates. Toss the Barrel at the blockade to gain access to the pair of SharpClaw in the pen. Once Fox defeats the duo, a large orange panel will appear above the door leading to Tricky.

Don't head after Tricky just yet; the rock wall at the end of the path has a large crack in it! Plant a Bomb Spore in the Planting Patch and shoot it with the Fire Blaster to gain access to a secret cave. In addition to a **Fuel Cell**, this particular cave contains the first of several **Cheat Wells** that can be found on Dinosaur Planet.

NOTE   FEELING CHEATED?

Nobody is quite certain as to what magical powers the Cheat Wells contain. Although legend states that if a Cheat Token is dropped into one of the Wells, and a wish is made, mystical, sage-like abilities will be revealed. However, Cheat Tokens can be purchased at the Cheat Well for 20 Scarabs apiece. Only one token can be bought from each Cheat Well. Once you've purchased a Cheat Token, take it to the WarpStone Maze.

Blast the orange panel with the Fire Blaster to gain access to the prison. Inside, Fox will find two SharpClaw soldiers jabbing at the young EarthWalker with their spiked clubs. During the commotion caused by Fox's appearance, Tricky runs off and the SharpClaw hop on separate SharpClaw Racers and chase after him. There's an extra SharpClaw Racer for Fox too—the race begins!

SHARPCLAW RACER CHALLENGE

SAVE AND CRASH   TIP

Once the cutscene ends, quickly press the ⬤ Button and save your progress. Jump back to the action and practice flying the racer. Once you get a feel for it, however, lose the race. Fox will restart back at the cave where the racer awaits. Don't get on it just yet! Instead, fetch the two Fuel Cells in the corners of the cave where Tricky was being harassed.

If Fox is to rescue the kidnapped Prince, he's got to beat the SharpClaw to the edge of Ice Mountain. If the SharpClaw get there first, Fox will slide out of control and the scene will have to be replayed.

Controlling the SharpClaw Racer is as simple as pressing the Ⓐ Button to accelerate and the Ⓑ Button to brake. Steering, of course, is done with the ⬤. We recommend keeping the Ⓐ Button depressed for all but the tightest of turns and, even then, the Ⓑ Button should be used sparingly. Although the racers hover off the ground, the depth of the snow does affect their speed. Try to stick to the icier patches as they allow for a faster ride.

1 Hop on the racer and go, go, go! Just after the first tunnel is a hard right turn. Watch out for the boulder lying in the middle of the path just beyond the turn.

2 Take the right-hand fork after the boulder, as this path is both faster and straighter. Cut the very wide hairpin turn that follows as tight as possible to gain ground.

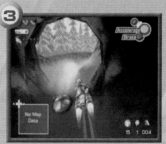

3 The SharpClaw will step up their efforts by tossing land mines in Fox's path. Be extra careful in the tunnels since there's little margin for error.

4 Just beyond the lengthy tunnel is a major fork. Follow the SharpClaw to the right. Although the left route is a shorter distance, the snow is far too deep to maintain adequate speed.

5 There's one final fork in the trail after the long, curvy downhill run. Once again, take the right-hand route. Be sure to keep a straight line, as the tunnel gets quite narrow.

6 Get ahead of the two SharpClaw before reaching the two trees forming an "X"— that's the end of the road!

The SharpClaw may be a bit brutish, but they know these hills well and know not to slide off the cliff. Fox, on the other hand, will careen out of control over the edge of the cliff and into a hot spring below. And it's a good thing too, since none other than Prince Tricky is there waiting at the water's edge for him. Fox will update the spunky royal about his father's capture and how badly his mother is worried about him.

En Route to SnowHorn Wastes

EVERYBODY NEEDS A SIDEKICK

MAP Ice Mountain-SnowHorn Wastes

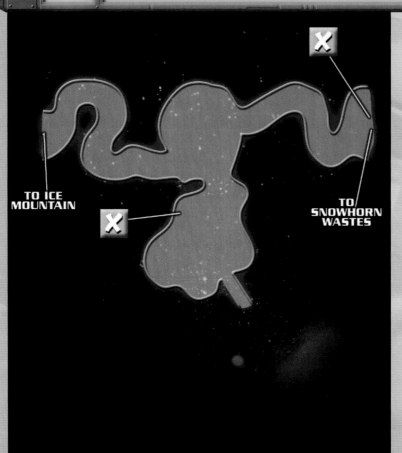

TO ICE
MOUNTAIN

TO
SNOWHORN
WASTES

Now that Fox has Prince Tricky in his care, he's got to bring the tike back home to his mom. Although Tricky does a good job of keeping up with Fox, he is still young and often needs some instruction. Fortunately, Tricky's dad has already trained him in what the lad likes to call his "Sidekick Commands". Tricky already knows the "Find Secret", "Stay", and "Heel" commands very well. Use the Ⓒ to select one of these commands from the blue panel in the inventory screen and press the Ⓐ Button to issue the command. For more information on Tricky's abilities, see the 'Sidekick Commands' section of the *Mission Basics* chapter.

NOTE I'm Hungry!

Dinosaurs have a voracious appetite and Tricky is no exception. Tricky's favorite snack is **Blue GrubTub Fungus**, but they're too difficult for him to catch. Every time Tricky performs one of his Sidekick Commands, he loses a little energy. Fox can carry up to 15 Blue GrubTub Fungi at once. Select them from the red panel in the inventory screen and feed them to Tricky to keep his energy levels high.

Follow the windy path through the snow to a large lava-filled pit. Fox will have to explore the area to the right of the pit in order to find a way across. Collect the two Blue GrubTubs down the path and feed them to Tricky.

Once Tricky has some energy, lead him over to the dried mud patch on the ground near the fire and select the "Find Secret" command. Tricky will start digging in the dirt and will reveal a panel in the ground. This panel controls a nearby gate. Stand atop the panel and select the "Stay" command to make Tricky sit down on the panel, thereby holding the gate open. Run through the open gate and use the Staff to flip the switch inside the cave. This will cause a stone pillar to rise in the lava pit, giving the pair a way to cross.

Climb down the rocks to the lava pit and jump across to the other side. Don't worry about Tricky; he'll catch up. Fox will encounter a seemingly impassable cliff beyond the lava pit. Fortunately, Tricky will spy a cracked area in the rock and will inform Fox that he thinks he knows a way out. Select the "Find Secret" command once again and watch as Tricky burrows through the base of the cliff. Crawl through the tunnel to reach SnowHorn Wastes.

BRINGING TRICKY HOME

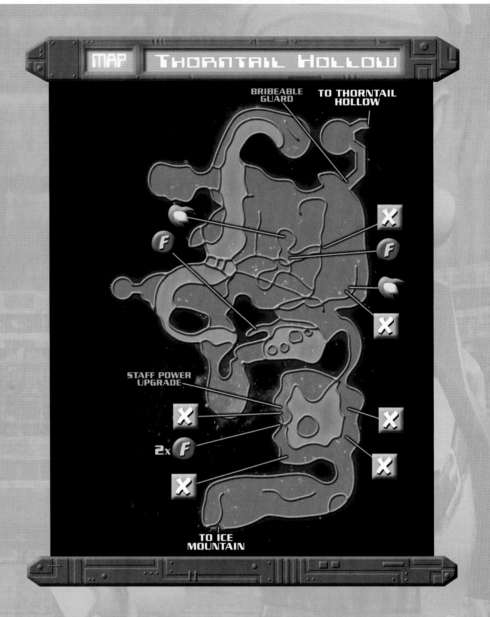

MAP Thorntail Hollow

BRIBEABLE GUARD

TO THORNTAIL HOLLOW

STAFF POWER UPGRADE

TO ICE MOUNTAIN

48

SnowHorn Wastes is crawling with SharpClaw and Fox doesn't have to go far before encountering them. Although he can easily defend the pair against their attackers, Tricky is still traumatized from being kidnapped and runs off down the path and straight into a SharpClaw camp! Beat down the SharpClaw and rush down the path towards the frozen lake up ahead. Get between Tricky and his pursuers and finish them off one at a time.

NOTE — NIGHTY, NIGHT

Depending on what time of day it is, the various dinosaurs may be asleep when Fox and Tricky encounter them. If night has already fallen, the SnowHorn may be sleeping when Fox reaches him. Look around the area and wait for sunrise in order to talk to him. Hitting the SnowHorn with the Staff will not get him to rise early, so be patient.

Gather up the Blue GrubTubs in the center of the lake and feed them to Tricky. Now that the threat of attack has been eliminated, start investigating the surroundings. A good way to start is by talking to the locals—there's a SnowHorn standing in the snow near the lake, but he says he's too hungry to talk to strangers right now. Fox and Tricky are going to have dig him up something to eat—literally.

Investigate the area along the west and south sides of the lake. Once there, Fox will be able to have Tricky dig up two **Alpine Roots** by issuing the "Find Secret" command. Take these roots back over to the SnowHorn to get him talking. After giving him the first Alpine Root, the SnowHorn will reward Fox with the **Small Scarab Bag**. It can hold up to 50 Scarabs!

The SnowHorn is obviously in a generous mood, and is still a bit hungry. Offer the second Alpine Root to him and watch as he freezes the geyser into a large block of ice. This block of ice can be pulled and pushed around the frozen lake by standing near it and holding down the Ⓐ Button. Push the block towards the northeast corner of the lake and climb onto it to reach the two **Fuel Cells** on the ledge.

You may notice that Fox's Staff is glowing green in this area. That's because one of the underground power-up locations is nearby! Jump down from the ledge and locate the dried patch of dirt near the log to the right. Issue the "Find Secret" command to have Tricky dig up the entrance to the cave below. Jump into the hole and head to the back of the cave to find the first **Staff Power Upgrade**.

NOTE — STOP AND GO

The entrances to the underground power-up caves will emit a green glow when there is an upgrade available. Once Fox has entered the cave and received its gifts, the glow will turn to red.

Grab hold of the ice block and push it clear across the ice towards the cliff to the right of the SnowHorn. Fox can then climb onto the ice block and hoist himself up onto the cliff to continue on through SnowHorn Wastes.

Once at the fork in the trail, climb up the hill onto the small clearing overlooking the pond on the left. A dragon-like creature will emerge from the snow so be ready! These creatures can quickly appear and disappear in the snow, but are worth defeating as they always drop an Energy Gem. Flip the switch on the wall to raise another platform in the pond.

Return to the main path and carefully hop across the pond towards the icy SnowHorn on the far shore. Although Fox won't perish if he falls into the water, he had better swim to the banks fast or else he'll quickly suffer damage. The bone-chilling water isn't the only hazard, however. The rocks along the left side of the pond house a family of bats that will fire projectiles at passersby. Keep moving to avoid the barrage. The SnowHorn will tell a woeful tale about someone stealing his Gold Root, but will offer no other information. Perhaps Fox can find this Gold Root at a later time?

Jump onto the recently raised platform and from there into the alcove east of the pond to find two **Fuel Cells**. Head back to the main path and continue down the hill. Once at the base of the mountain, turn to the left and locate the dried patch of dirt near the cliffs in the corner. Here, Tricky will be able to dig up a **BafomDad**. These miraculous creatures can be used to restore life to their captors. So long as Fox has a BafomDad in his possession, he will have the opportunity to "Continue" his journey from wherever he is when he falls dead.

Bafom-WHAT? — TIP

A BafomDad is essentially a "Continue". Whenever Fox dies you will be instantly presented with a screen that asks whether or not you want to continue. By selecting "yes" Fox will be brought back to life with full life. However, by selecting "no" you will be forced to continue the journey from the last place game progress was saved. The tricky part to all of this is that the Continue Screen appears instantly. It's very easy to confirm the default selection of "no" with an accidental press of the Ⓐ Button—especially if Fox should perish during a heated battle! When running low on energy, it's best to be very deliberate with each press of the Ⓐ Button so as to reduce the risk of an unwanted menu selection.

Smash the cask in the far back corner of this area to find an orange Scarab. This is the rarest and most elusive of Scarabs and is equal in value to ten green Scarabs.

There is a crack in the rocks directly across from the path that Fox and Tricky descended. Put Tricky to work by giving him his "Find Secret" command. Crawl through the resulting tunnel to enter a cave containing a **Fuel Cell** and a SharpClaw Crate with a **BafomDad** in it. Exit the cave and talk to the roaming SnowHorns to learn of their captured leader. These SharpClaw sure do love to kidnap dinosaurs!

Fox will encounter a locked gate and a seemingly guarded tunnel up ahead. Approach the sentry near the tunnel and press the Ⓐ Button to find out that this particular BribeClaw can be bribed for a mere 25 Scarabs. Search the area for boulders and use the Ⓐ Button to pry them up to collect all the Scarabs you can. Give the Scarabs to the guard by selecting them from the red panel of the inventory screen and pressing the Ⓐ Button. The guard will then step aside, allowing Fox and Tricky to continue on towards ThornTail Hollow.

Follow the corridor to the circular room and quickly duck into the hall to the right; the flaming bats are immune to the Fire Blaster's attacks! Continue on to the sewers ahead.

ThornTail Sewers

A Short Swim From Home

Follow the windy corridor to the sewers. The current is flowing counter-clockwise and it's just too strong for Fox and Tricky to swim against so they're going to have to reverse it. Swim to the platform near the sewer grate and have Tricky "Stay" on the large panel. This will allow Fox to climb the wall and pass through the gate above. The gated ledge above the sewers contains a switch. Flip the switch and then jump back in the water with Tricky to finish the journey to ThornTail Hollow. During the first visit here, the current flows in the proper direction. However, from then on it does not.

Tricky will waist no time in running off to let his mom know he's all right. Hurry back to the temple where Fox last saw the Queen to find out what the next objective is.

SPELLSTONE #1

FINDING THE FIRST SPELLSTONE

Fox may have thought that rescuing Tricky was all he had to do to complete the mission, but as Peppy Hare quickly reminds him, the planet is not back together yet! To make matters worse, Queen EarthWalker has fallen ill. Perhaps if Fox can help cure her, she'll be able to help him begin reassembling the planet? The first piece of this puzzle is DarkIce Mines, but in order to get there, Fox is going to have to find the GateKeeper.

THORNTAIL HOLLOW

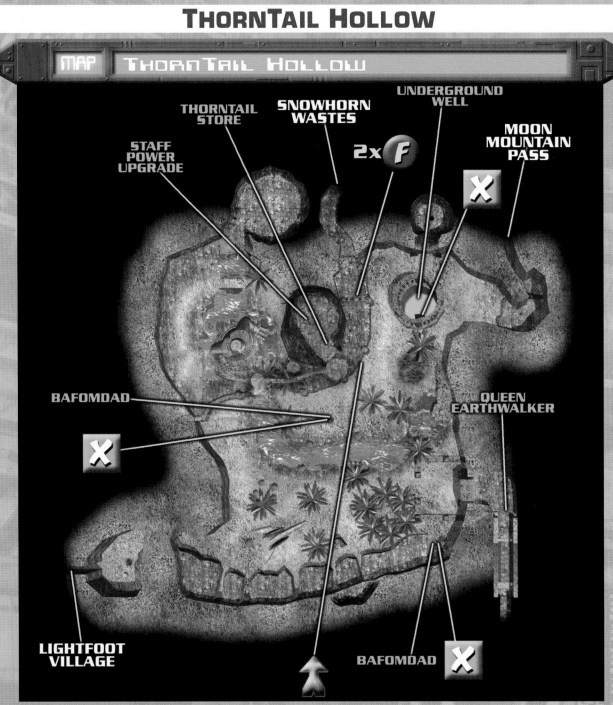

MAP | ThornTail Hollow

CURING THE QUEEN

If Tricky's hunch is right, his mom is only going to get better if they can bring her some White GrubTubs. Let the Queen rest and head outside to search the Hollow for the special fungus. Although finding the White GrubTubs is very important, Fox will benefit by having Tricky dig in each of the dried dirt patches found throughout the area. The first of these is near the ThornTail just south of the temple entrance. There, Tricky can dig up a **BafomDad**!

Taking the time to talk to the ThornTails that live in the Hollow will net Fox some clues as to where the White GrubTub may be found. Although many will simply express their concern for the Queen's well being others will hint at a large underground well being the perfect environment for White GrubTubs.

Since underground caves tend to be quite dark, it's a good idea for Fox to purchase the **FireFly Lantern** (20 Scarabs) ahead of time. Also, since Fox is likely to want to carry multiple BafomDads (there's another **BafomDad** buried out front of the ThornTail Store) he should buy the **BafomDad Holder** (20 Scarabs) as well.

Leave the shop and approach the large circular structure to the east. Give Tricky his "Find Secret" command and stand back and watch him burrow through the crack in the structure's façade. Behold, the entrance to the well the ThornTails had mentioned!

THORNTAIL WELL

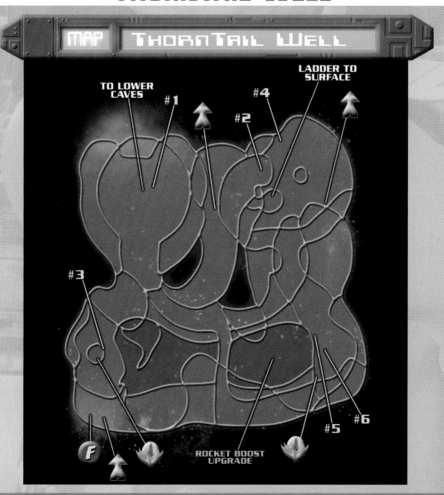

MAP — THORNTAIL WELL

TO LOWER CAVES
LADDER TO SURFACE
#1 #4 #2
#3
#5 #6
ROCKET BOOST UPGRADE

COLLECTING WHITE GRUBTUBS

I'm Going In!   TIP

Fox is going to need several Bomb Spores and FireFlies in order to reach the White GrubTubs. Be sure to gather up these items before entering the well to keep from having to backtrack later on.

It's a long way down into the well so Tricky will have to stay at the surface. Descend the lengthy ladder all the way to the bottom and sneak past the poisonous red mushrooms to the adjacent room. Plant a Bomb Spore in the Planting Patch in the center of the pond and detonate it with the Fire Blaster to reveal an underground power-up location.

This secret area contains the **Rocket Boost Upgrade**. With this special ability, Fox will be able to use the Staff to leap to unimaginable heights. When standing on a Rocket Boost Pad, select the Rocket Boost from the yellow panel in the inventory screen and hold down the Ⓐ Button to charge the Staff. Once fully charged, the Staff will blast upward into the air, delivering Fox to the next reachable ledge.

Return to the area near the bottom of the ladder and seek out the Rocket Boost Pad. Put Fox's new power to use on the pad and leap to the upper ledge. Head through the archway to the room with the water and plant a Bomb Spore in the Planting Patch on the rock bridge. Shoot the Bomb Spore Plant to cause an explosion that drops a cube-shaped piece of rock onto the ground below.

Jump down after the block and push it onto the large black switch at the end of the cave. The square boulder is more than heavy enough to hold the nearby gate open.

Stop, Drop, Roll   TIP

Fox will often suffer one block of damage when falling too far. However, if you press the Button right before impact, Fox will tuck and roll during the landing, thereby preventing any injury. It takes some practice to get the timing down, but this little trick can save valuable energy later in the adventure!

Don't go through the gate just yet; smash the SharpClaw Crate in the southwest corner to reveal a secret Rocket Boost Pad. Use this Pad to reach the two **Fuel Cells** on the ledge above.

Shoot the Bomb Spore Plant on the rock pedestal near the black switch to stock up on Bomb Spores and then head through the gate to the northwestern corner of the well. The ThornTail in this room will only cooperate if Fox has the FireFly Lantern. If he deems Fox prepared to enter the "lower sanctum," he'll happily step off the Bomb Spore Planting Patch so Fox can continue.

Detonate a Bomb Spore where the ThornTail was napping and descend the ladder to the dank, dark, caves below. Fox isn't far from the White GrubTub now!

1 The first **White GrubTub** is hopping around near the base of the ladder. Stun it with the Staff and scoop it up while it's dazed.

2 Follow the caves around to the left and use the Rocket Boost to reach the upper ledge. There Fox can snag a **White GrubTub** as well as some **FireFlies**.

3 Let a FireFly loose and enter the pitch-black cave across from the Rocket Boost Pad. Use a Bomb Spore to blow through the cave wall to find the next **White GrubTub**.

4 Follow the main corridor to the pool at the end and descend the long dark slope off to the left to the next **White GrubTub**.

5-6 Detonate a Bomb Spore near the rock column by #4 and return to #2. Fox can now jump across the void and reach the final two **White GrubTubs** on the other side.

55

C'mon, Fox, we'll make a great team!

Now that Fox has all the White GrubTubs he needs, reunite with Tricky on the surface and hurry off to give the mushrooms to the Queen. Once rejuvenated, the Queen will provide Fox with all the information he needs. She explains to him the purpose of the four SpellStones and the Force Point Temples. She elaborates on General Scales' unprecedented strengths. And, for better or for worse, she decrees that Tricky shall accompany Fox throughout his journey to find the SpellStones.

Queen EarthWalker received word from her spies that General Scales was last seen heading to DarkIce Mines. To get there, Fox will need to talk with Garunda Te, the GateKeeper to that world. Take the **SharpClaw Prison Key** from the Queen and head back outside; Fox has to get to SnowHorn Wastes! Travel back to the sewers to enter SnowHorn Wastes.

SNOWHORN WASTES

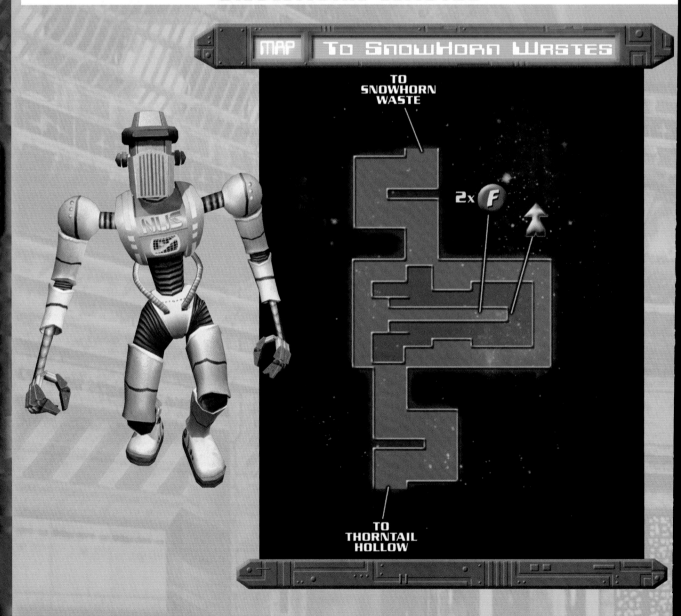

MAP   To SnowHorn Wastes

TO SNOWHORN WASTE

2x F

TO THORNTAIL HOLLOW

HAS ANYBODY SEEN GARUNDA TE?

Chances are that the current in the sewers is going to need to be redirected again. Make Tricky "Stay" on the black panel while Fox climbs up the wall and flips the switch on the ledge. Don't rush the swim to the other side. On the inside of the hairpin turn is a Rocket Boost Pad. Rocket up to the upper ledge and then use the Fire Blaster to shoot the orange panel high on the wall to open the gate to the two **Fuel Cells**.

Exit the sewers and cross the snowy field outside the tunnel to the large gate. Insert the SharpClaw Prison Key in the hole to the left of the gate to gain access to the prison yard. Head up the hill to the left and approach the hole in the center of the ice to talk to Garunda Te.

Garunda Te has been imprisoned in the bottom of an icy cave with nothing but a breathe-hole for his trunk. Fox and Tricky are going to have to work together to bring him three Frost Weeds so he'll have the strength to bust out of his icy jail.

The **Frost Weeds** Garunda Te requires are hanging from the nearby tree; the only problem is that a half dozen SharpClaw are going to mount a big attack in hopes of squelching Garunda's escape plans! Thwack the tree with the Staff to knock the Frost Weeds to the ground and quickly give Tricky his "Find Secret" command. This will allow Fox to busy himself with the SharpClaw while Tricky delivers the Frost Weeds to Garunda Te.

NOTE — GARUNDA'S METER

The meter that appears on the bottom of the screen indicates Garunda Te's strength. Once it's filled up, he will have enough strength to bust through the icy ceiling in his cell. It takes three Frost Weeds to max out his meter.

Keep a close eye on Tricky to make sure he's kicking the Frost Weeds up the hill to where Garunda can reach them. Some of the Frost Weeds may roll too far down the hill, so be sure to smack the tree again once Tricky comes back. Fox can help deliver the Frost Weeds too; just kick one up the hill by running into it. Garunda Te will suck it up with his trunk once the Frost Weed hits the ice.

Once Garunda Te breaks free, and the SharpClaw scatter, he'll tell the story of how he was captured and of the horrible fate befallen on the SnowHorn Tribe. The mighty SnowHorn wants nothing more than the return of the SpellStone and happily opens the Gate to DarkIce Mines. When Fox finds the SpellStone, he must then deliver it to the Volcano Force Point Temple in order for the powers of the SpellStone to take effect.

Although Peppy and Slippy may be trying to get Fox to hurry back to the Arwing, there's some exploring that needs to be done first. Head down the hill past the tree towards the icy river on the left and ride one of the floating ice patches all the way downstream. There, Fox will find another **Cheat Token Well**.

From the Well, head up the narrow path to the left to find a **Fuel Cell** sitting out in the open above the river. Jump down off the ledge and enter the cave. Use the Fire Blaster to fend off the underground monsters that pop out of the floor and have Tricky dig up the **BafomDad** buried in the center of the cave. Shoot the orange panel near the ceiling to make an additional two **Fuel Cells** appear outside the cave on the ledge.

With the rest of these items in his possession, Fox is ready to return to ThornTail Hollow and prepare for his trip to DarkIce Mines.

ThornTail Hollow

Preparing for Liftoff

Once back in the Hollow, put the Rocket Boost ability to use and leap to the roof of the ThornTail Store. Use the Rocket Boost Pad near the Store entrance and grab the two **Fuel Cells** off to the right. Plant a Bomb Spore in the Planting Patch near the cracked rock wall. Blast the Plant and enter the cave that appears. Shoot the four orange panels inside the cave to trigger the appearance of an underground power-up location. Inside, Fox will gain another **Staff Power Upgrade**.

Take the time to fill up the Scarab Bag near the circle of rocks and head to the ThornTail Store—it's time to go shopping! The upcoming journey will be made easier if Fox purchases the **DarkIce Mines Map** (5 Scarabs) and **Hi-Def Display** (20 Scarabs). Also, since it's apparent that Tricky is going to be tagging along for a while, it wouldn't hurt to pick up something little for him to play with. Spend another 15 Scarabs and buy **Tricky's Ball** for him; the ShopKeeper apparently gets most of his wares by stealing from the royals!

Been Caught Stealing TIP

The ShopKeeper has hidden many of his Scarabs in casks on a second level ledge in the map room. Cross the room to the hall in the back and search the left-hand corner for a Rocket Boost Pad. Rocket up to the balcony and smash the casks in the nearby room to lay claim to the ShopKeeper's private stash!

NOTE Let's Play!

You've no doubt heard Tricky ask Fox to play. Well, it's time to accommodate the boy. Gather up some more Scarabs from the circle of rocks and purchase Tricky's Ball from the ShopKeeper for 15 Scarabs. Whenever Tricky yells out, "Let's play!" select the ball from the inventory screen and press the Ⓐ Button to toss it. Play fetch often enough and Tricky might just surprise you one day.

Fox is now ready to make the trip to DarkIce Mines. Head back to the Arwing and press the Ⓐ Button to board the craft.

59

SPACE TRAVEL

DESTINATION: DARKICE MINES

Fuel Cells Needed: 5

Gold Rings: 3 of 10

Time: 1:00

The route to DarkIce Mines is strewn with Arwing-crushing asteroids and mines. Fox is going to need quick reflexes in order to survive the journey in one piece.

NOTE — **GOING FOR GOLD**

Follow the directions to pick up the Gold Rings in the order that they appear. This way, the remaining 7 Gold Rings can act as backups in case any of the first 3 Gold Rings are missed.

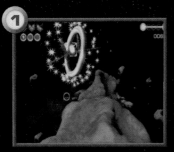

1 Avoid the first few asteroids and watch for the Silver Ring that appears. The first Gold Ring is just beyond the Silver Ring, but slightly lower in the sky.

2 The second Gold Ring is just off the surface of the first island. Fly through the first archway and keep to the left when going past the smaller, second arch. The Gold Ring is just beyond it.

3 Swoop down into the tiny canyon on the second island and blast through the Silver Ring and the Special Crate to get a line on the next Gold Ring.

The Gold Rings get slightly more difficult to fly through beyond this first group. Expect to encounter moving Gold Rings, as well as one with a yellow and red "X" in the center of it. Blast at the "X" with the Arwing's laser cannon in order to open it up.

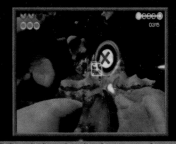

DARKICE MINES

OUT IN THE COLD

MAP DARKICE MINES

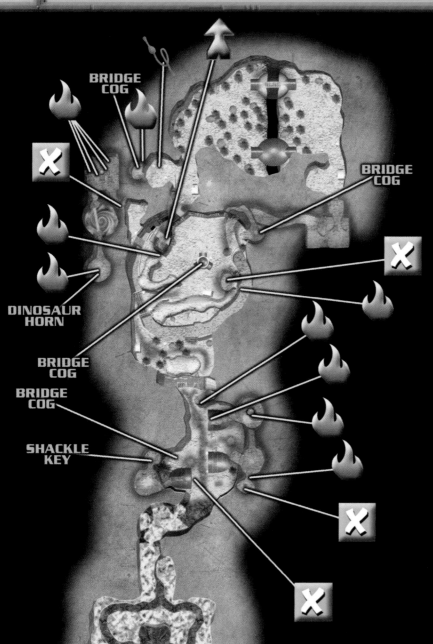

BRIDGE
COG

BRIDGE
COG

DINOSAUR
HORN

BRIDGE
COG

BRIDGE
COG

SHACKLE
KEY

61

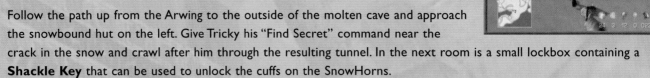

Although it may not seem like it from the fiery pit where Fox lands the Arwing, the surface of DarkIce Mines is a bitter cold, snow-covered land best left to the SnowHorn Tribe. Fox and Tricky are going to brave the elements if they're to find a way down into the mines where the SnowHorns, particularly Garunda Te's daughter, have been enslaved.

Follow the path up from the Arwing to the outside of the molten cave and approach the snowbound hut on the left. Give Tricky his "Find Secret" command near the crack in the snow and crawl after him through the resulting tunnel. In the next room is a small lockbox containing a **Shackle Key** that can be used to unlock the cuffs on the SnowHorns.

Crawl back through the snow tunnel and head around the side of the hut to free the SnowHorn with the Shackle Key. In return for your efforts, the SnowHorn will offer up a **Bridge Cog**. She also asks that Fox and Tricky keep an eye out for Belina Te, Garunda's daughter. Stop and talk to the other SnowHorns in this area and head through the archway towards the waterfall.

Drop off the cliff and onto the wooden walkway near the water. There's a machine behind the cascading water that has an empty spindle. Place the Bridge Cog on the machine and flip the lever to extend a bridge across the river. Climb the rocks back to the upper ledge and cross the bridge with Tricky.

Follow the path around to where two SharpClaw are mercilessly beating on an injured SnowHorn. Rush to the aid of the SnowHorn by defeating the SharpClaw with a series of swift combinations from the Staff. Once the SharpClaw are extinguished, the SnowHorn will coax Tricky into trying out his "Flame" ability. With this new talent, Tricky can melt plates of ice, as well as start fires! The SnowHorn is willing to be of further assistance, but he needs some food.

NOTE — TRICKY'S FLAME

Tricky packs quite a punch with that Flame of his. Fox had better stand clear when having Tricky use his newest Sidekick Command as the flames can do as much as three blocks of damage to Fox! Fox isn't the only one whose fur might get singed; Tricky can be told to Flame SharpClaws as well!

Return to the area where the huts and SnowHorns were and use Tricky's "Flame" command to melt the two ice walls near the archway. The one in the rock wall merely leads to an Energy Gem near the waterfall, whereas the other leads into an abandoned SharpClaw hut.

Enter the hut and have Tricky light the pile of wood on fire. This will cause the icy floor to melt, revealing a secret tunnel in the floor. Drop through the hole to reach an underground cave and have Tricky "Flame" the icy panel in the rear wall. Feed Tricky the GrubTubs off to the side to replenish the boy's energy and then give him his "Find Secret" orders to dig up the **Alpine Root** buried in the ground.

Push the large block back towards the hole and climb up onto it to exit the caves.

If Fox is to ever get some help from the weary SnowHorn, he's going to have to find some more food—one Alpine Root just doesn't cut it when you weigh two tons! Head down the slope to the icy chute where the boulders are being rolled. Dodge the boulders while running up the slope towards them and have Tricky melt the ice-covered entrance to the cave on the left. Once inside, give Tricky the "Find Secret" command to have him dig up a second **Alpine Root**.

Once the SnowHorn is fed he'll allow Fox to climb onto his back. Use the nearby platform to mount the beast and steer him towards the barred gate across the bridge. Press the (A) Button to perform the Tusk Attack and continue on into the SharpClaw base camp up ahead. Guide the SnowHorn to the platform on the right and press the (A) Button to dismount.

Although most of the SharpClaw are sound asleep inside the hut, there is one manning a cannon directly above the Life-Force Door (defeat five enemies to open). Cross the yard to the ice wall by the tunnel and have Tricky melt it.

Dash through the tunnel to escape the cannon's bombardment and then climb the ladder on the right to enter the machine room. Fox is going to have to find three more Bridge Cogs in order to get this bridge to work. For now, use the Rocket Boost to leap to the upper ledge. Hop from platform to rickety platform on the other side of the rock walls to reach the SharpClaw at the cannon.

Just as Fox defeats the lone watchman, daylight will break and the SharpClaw troops will begin going on the attack. Quickly top off the Staff Energy Meter with the nearby Magical Plant and step up to the cannon. Press the (A) Button to take control of the cannon. Use the (O) to aim and the (A) Button to fire. The longer the (A) Button is depressed, the further the cannonballs will fly. The first two SharpClaw will appear to the left of the hut. Lob a couple of short cannonballs on them and then focus on the two sneaking along the back wall of the area. Use the cannon to polish off the fifth and final SharpClaw to break the seal on the Life-Force Door. But don't stop there, fire one final cannonball through the boarded up cave entrance in the far right-hand corner.

63

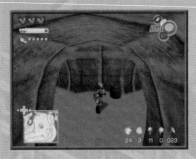

Jump down from the ledge and enter the cave below to gain a **Bridge Cog** from the lockbox. Leave the cave and enter the SharpClaw's hut to find another **Bridge Cog**. There's one more Cog needed to get the machine working. Enter the cave that was previously boarded up and climb the hill on the left towards the four torches. Have Tricky melt the ice wall by the rocks and enter the cave to find the final **Bridge Cog**. Return to the machine room and place all three Cogs on the spindles and pull the lever to activate the bridge.

Run across the bridge and up the slope towards the muddy wall with the crack in it. Give Tricky the "Find Secret" command and stand back as he burrows a tunnel into the room on the other side.

TAKING A LEAP OF FAITH

This torch-lit room contains a plaque that reads, "Beyond the leap of faith lies an ancient prize". In order to gain access to the mystical area where this leap of faith takes place, Fox has to complete a puzzle.

1 Stand at the rear of the room and use the Fire Blaster to shoot the orange panel near the ceiling at the back of the room.

2 The duo has 60 seconds to ignite a fire hot enough to trigger the opening of the door. Guide Tricky to each of the four red grates in the center of the room and give him his "Flame" command.

3 Go through the doorway near the plaque and take a running leap into the abyss. Fox will land on a glittery, narrow, walkway. Cross the magical bridge to the cave on the other side.

4 Have Tricky use his "Flame" ability one more time to melt the block of ice in this room. This will allow Fox to lay claim to the **Dinosaur Horn**.

OUT IN THE COLD PART 2

With the Dinosaur Horn in his possession, Fox is now ready to make the final push for the underground mines. Return to the SharpClaw camp and continue on through the previously boarded-up cave towards the hilltop with the four torches. Stand between the torches and blow the Dinosaur Horn to summon a SnowHorn.

Mount the SnowHorn and ride him out into the blizzard. In order to make it through the storm, Fox needs to make sure the SnowHorn gets plenty of Alpine Roots along the way. Luckily, there's a lengthy trail of Alpine Roots that not only keep the SnowHorn from succumbing to the elements, but they lead right towards the mines! Follow the Alpine Roots across the bridge and out of the storm. Once near the unloading platform, Fox will realize that Tricky has gone astray. Ride the SnowHorn over to the wooden gate and use his Tusk Attack to smash it to pieces.

NOTE | FOREVER LOST

Fox can run back out into the storm in search of Tricky, but a cinematic will show him returning, alone, after some time. Let's hope the SnowHorn is right when he said that Tricky would show up sooner or later.

Enter the cave that the SnowHorn made accessible and defeat the two SharpClaw to satisfy the requirements of the Life-Force Door. Hop aboard the SharpClaw Racer by the door to take a ride back across the snowfields and into General Scales' underground mines.

65

THE FIERY UNDERGROUND

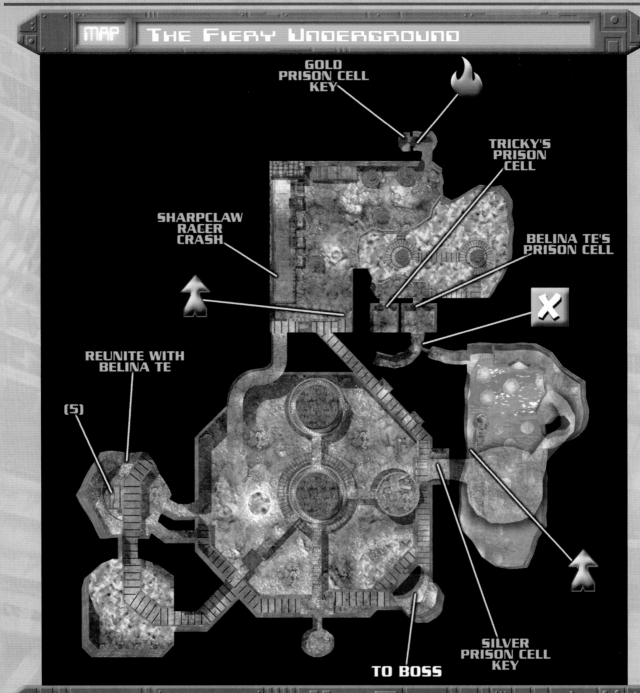

MAP THE FIERY UNDERGROUND

GOLD
PRISON CELL
KEY

TRICKY'S
PRISON
CELL

SHARPCLAW
RACER
CRASH

BELINA TE'S
PRISON CELL

REUNITE WITH
BELINA TE

(5)

SILVER
PRISON CELL
KEY

TO BOSS

Fox's SharpClaw Racer will eventually skid out of control and dump him onto a conveyor belt—a conveyor moving straight towards a series of four flame jets! Run against the belt's direction until the flame jets stop and then allow the belt to carry Fox past. Immediately start running again to avoid the next flame. Although there are Energy Gems near some of the flame jets, trying to nab them is an unnecessary risk.

Once at the end of the conveyor belt, step off to the right before getting pushed into the three vertical flames. Once on solid ground, Fox will be met by three SharpClaw soldiers. These particular SharpClaw are not only poorly armed, but they aren't very well trained in combat either. Fox can dispatch of them quite easily and when he does, a nearby Life-Force Door will open.

NOTE WHERE'S TRICKY WHEN YOU NEED HIM?

The Life-Force Door was blocking access to a small icy cave that requires Tricky's "Flame" command to get through.

Across the mine from the SnowHorn in the wheel is a Rocket Boost Pad. Rocket up to the ledge above and crawl through the small opening on the right. Wait for a boulder to pass and then run down the slope to the left after it. There are two alcoves along this track that Fox can duck into to regain some lost energy, but don't touch the walls, they're hot!

Head all the way to the end of the track and turn and face the alcove on the left. Shoot the orange panel on the wall with the Fire Blaster to extinguish the flame. This will allow Fox to open the lockbox and get the **Silver Prison Cell Key**. It's time to bust Tricky out of the slammer; return the way you came and approach the elevated walkways near the flaming towers.

Unlike most of the other flame jets encountered thus far, these don't periodically turn off. They do, however, rotate around a central tower, providing enough time for Fox to slip by. Carefully run across the walkway and clockwise around each of the two towers to reach the rocky ledge near the prison cells. Use the Silver Prison Cell Key in the second lock (the silver one) to free Tricky. Once the gate opens, rush in and give the young Prince some GrubTubs, he's starving!

HIGH JUMPING   TIP

Since the revolving flames and broken walkways make for a rough trip back the way you came, approach the gap in the handrail and jump down to the walkway below. Time this move right after a flame passes by and Fox won't get singed!

Enter the snowy cave where the Life-Force Door was and have Tricky melt the panel of ice so Fox can get the **Gold Prison Cell Key** from the lockbox. Return to the two prison cells and use the Key to free Belina Te. Upon hearing that Fox wasn't sent to rescue her, Belina gets so mad she rampages straight through the back of her cell, thereby revealing a hidden tunnel!

Belina Te promises to meet up with Fox and Tricky at the bottom of the mine; they must go on without her for now. Give Tricky his "Find Secret" command to have him burrow through the crack in the side of the tunnel. Crawl through the tunnel to reach an icy cavern containing a large lake and waterfall.

Fox has to reach the platform on the other side of the lake, but the water's too cold to swim in and the banks are too high. Draw the Staff and use the Fire Blaster ability to blast the three green-colored stalactites on the ceiling. Hop across the floating stalactites to the ledge with the switch and use the Staff in it to open the gate at the mouth of the stream.

Use the Rocket Boost Pad at the base of the cliff to leap to the edge of the stream above the waterfall. Take out the flying baddies with the Fire Blaster and then carefully hop across the floating patches of ice to reach the tunnel on the far side. The current is faster in the middle of the stream, so time the jump to the second ice patch well to avoid taking a chilly dip in the water. Enter the U-shaped

tunnel across the river and follow it to the square block of ice. Fox must push this block off the cliff so the duo can enter the cave below.

Jump down to the ledge made by the fallen ice block and call for Tricky. Lead the boy down the spiraling path to the lower area of the mines. Eliminate the SharpClaw by the campfire and bust open the SharpClaw Crates in the corner to replenish any lost energy.

Step onto the conveyor belt and cautiously run past the series of flame jets to the circular pathway in the distance. Descend further into the mines along this path to meet up with Belina Te. Belina doesn't quite know where the SpellStone is, but she knows you're getting close.

Head out onto the floor of the mines and clear away the SharpClaws there with a steady stream of combination attacks delivered straight to their noggin. Locate the ladder in the center of chamber, between the two rock towers, and climb up.

A TAIL OF TWO TOWERS

Fox is going to need the extra firepower of a **Fuel Barrel** in order to continue his quest through DarkIce Mines. Although there is one at the top of the ladder, delivering it to where he needs it is no small task.

1 Grab the Fuel Barrel and carry it up the spiraling walkway while stepping around the endless series of barrels. Each of the barrels follows a set path that consists of three bounces on the inside of the walkway and then three bounces along the outer edge. Pause momentarily as the barrel bounces by so as to step aside at the last second if need be. Save your progress when you reach the top of the spiral!

2 Once at the top, cross the bridge to the other tower and gently place the Fuel Barrel down on the pad opposite the ladder.

3 Climb the ladder and use the Staff to flip the switch. A magnetic lift will float down and transport the barrel to the upper walkway.

4 Grab the Fuel Barrel and carry it across the upper bridge to the original tower. Tiptoe past each of the flame jets—remember, those are explosives Fox is carrying—and cross the bridge towards the crack in the rock wall. Toss the Fuel Barrel at the crack to reveal a secret cave. Flip the switch and save your progress.

5 Descend the ladders and cross the bridge at the top of the spiral (where the barrels appear). Follow the chute through several caves to another switch. This one controls the upper bridge.

6 Return to the upper portion of the towers and climb the ladder near the green torches to reach the SharpClaw Cannon. Use the Cannon to shoot at the two wooden X's on the tower straight ahead and the one to the right. This will cause a stone platform to appear leading out of the mines. Phew!

THE FIERY UNDERGROUND PART 2

Descend the ladders and spiraling walkway to the ground below and reunite with Tricky. Bust open the SharpClaw Crates littering the ground to fill up on energy and cross the stone bridge to the cave on the other side. Stand atop the Warp Pad and press the Ⓐ Button to enter the realm of Galdon, the boss of DarkIce Mines.

BOSS FIGHT: GALDON

Fox and Tricky are so close to finding the first SpellStone, they can almost taste it! Unfortunately, there's one rather large hurdle remaining in their way: Galdon, the ruler of DarkIce Mines! This battle takes place in four phases, the first of which requires good teamwork between Tricky and Fox. Make sure Tricky has been fed all the Blue GrubTubs he can stomach, and that both of Fox's energy meters are full as well.

Approach the enormous, ice-encrusted beast and have Tricky use his "Flame" command. This will melt the ice and awake the monstrous creature from his slumber. Although Tricky is quick to notice the SpellStone in the creature's mitts, Galdon senses the duo's desires and swallows the SpellStone. Fox didn't come this far to have some prehistoric reptile swallow the SpellStone—the fight is on!

Galdon is completely covered in a thick layer of armor and is not susceptible to damage from Fox's measly Staff, with one exception: his tail! Despite being much, much bigger than Fox and Tricky, Galdon is quite agile and will work hard to continuously face Fox so that his tail is never vulnerable to attack. Fox must create a diversion if he's to ever get access to that tail.

ATTACK PHASE 1

During this first phase of the battle, Galdon will rely on a green fiery attack (two blocks of damage) and the occasional flames that roar up through the vents for protection. In addition, the beast will try to crash his body and head down onto Fox whenever possible. Anytime Fox comes into contact with Galdon's armor, Fox loses one block of energy.

NOTE   MIGHTY TASTY

The SharpClaw Crates and GrubTubs found throughout Galdon's area will reappear over time. After each phase of the battle, or whenever Fox has suffered damage, flee to the edge of the room and chow down on some tasty DumbleDang Pods. Be sure to give Tricky some GrubTubs too; keeping energy levels high is the key to winning this battle.

Assign Tricky's "Flame" command to the ⓐ Button and charge towards Galdon's torso. Give Tricky the "go ahead" to torch the beast's chest and quickly run under his legs to get behind him. Tricky's flame won't dish out any damage, but it is enough of a diversion to get Fox a clean shot at Galdon's tail. If you don't want to suck up your GrubTub supply, giving Tricky the "Stay" command will also work.

Quickly launch into a combination attack aimed at the glowing tip of the tail. Although the tail will recoil briefly out of Fox's reach, keep swinging the Staff and don't stop. It only takes **three hits** to permanently injure Galdon.

ATTACK PHASE 2

Galdon doesn't appreciate Fox's attacks on his backside and promptly turns around and swallows the pint-sized adventurer whole. The second portion of this battle takes place inside Galdon, where Fox sees that the SpellStone has become imbedded in the creature's uvula.

Fox is free from harm during this phase (we can only hope the same for Tricky.) Whenever Fox is ready, he can unleash a devastating combination attack on the transparent uvula. If Fox waits too long, he'll be spit out and will need to begin Attack Phase 1 again. Fox only needs to land one of these combinations with the Staff to give Galdon the worst case of indigestion he's ever felt. Fox will be spat back out onto the ground after the successful combination.

ATTACK PHASE 3

As Fox regains his balance, he notices that Tricky's flame attack had done some damage after all: Galdon now has a large slash in his chest! Move to the edge of the room and assign the Fire Blaster to the 🔘 Button. Draw the Fire Blaster and hold down the 🔘 Button to be able to strafe left to right while keeping a watchful eye on Galdon's movements.

Dodge the green fiery attacks and his screeching neck thrust and wait for the gash in his chest to open. As soon as Galdon opens his chest to suck in the magical power from the air, Fox must rattle off several shots from the Fire Blaster. A blue glow will radiate outward from the beast's chest if Fox lands a clean hit. Fox must use his Fire Blaster to land **three hits** on Galdon's chest.

ATTACK PHASE 4

After being hit twice in the chest, Galdon decides to once again swallow Fox. This phase of the battle is the last and Fox doesn't need to hold anything back; he can unload every ounce of Staff Power he has on Galdon's swinging uvula with the Fire Blaster! Eventually the SpellStone and Fox will be regurgitated back onto the ground and Galdon will fall dead.

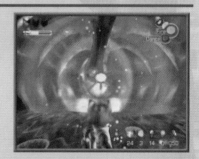

With Galdon a thing of the past, and the **Fire SpellStone** safely in Fox's possession, he and Tricky are set to return to Dinosaur Planet. Bid farewell to Belina Te and hop aboard the Arwing for the journey back to ThornTail Hollow. General Peppers will congratulate the duo on their efforts and will indicate that the Force Point Temple that this SpellStone needs to be returned to is just beyond Moon Mountain Pass.

> **NOTE** ┃ FLYING HOME
>
> The flight back to Dinosaur Planet is always the same: no Fuel Cells are consumed and the Arwing only needs to be flown through 1 Gold Ring to open the Force Field. See the first *ThornTail Hollow* chapter for tips on Gold Ring locations.

DELIVERING THE FIRST SPELLSTONE

THORNTAIL HOLLOW

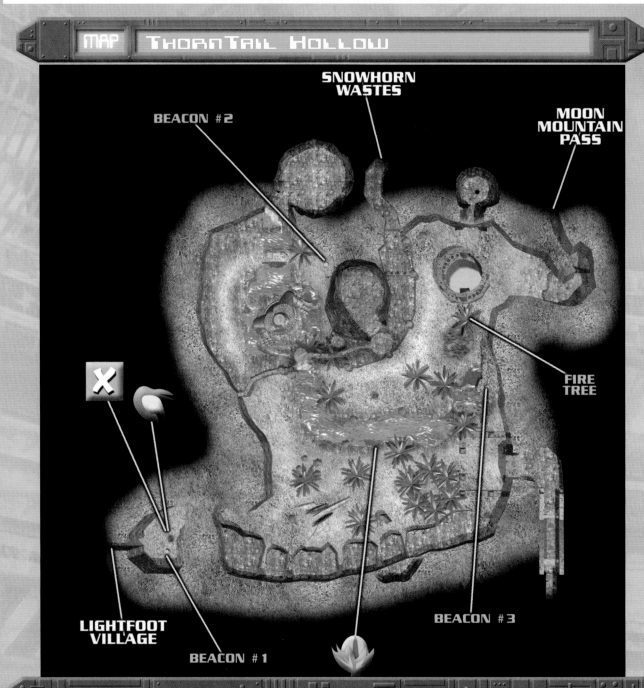

MAP ThornTail Hollow

SNOWHORN WASTES

BEACON #2

MOON MOUNTAIN PASS

FIRE TREE

LIGHTFOOT VILLAGE

BEACON #1

BEACON #3

LIGHTING THE BEACONS

No sooner does Fox step out of the Arwing before a ThornTail hurries up to bemoan the loss of their precious beacons. Well, the beacons are still there, but those dastardly SharpClaw have put out the flames and the ThornTails are scared of the dark! Fox must help them!

NOTE | Notice Anything Different?

By defeating Galdon and returning to Dinosaur Planet with the missing SpellStone, Fox has gained a fourth Energy Badge! Fox will earn additional Energy Badges each time he finds a SpellStone.

Although Tricky has an amazing flame, Fox needs to find something that will burn for a while. After all, he and Tricky can't keep the beacons burning all night; they've got to get to the Volcano Force Point Temple!

Located between the ancient well and the stream is a large tree with burning branches known as the Fire Tree. Give the tree a good whack with the Staff to knock loose some of its flaming branches. Rush up to one of the branches and extinguish its flame by hitting it with the Staff. Fox can safely pick up the **Fire Weed** once its flame is out. Each Fire Weed is able to keep a single beacon burning throughout the night; therefore you'll need three. As chance would have it, there are three beacons in the Hollow that need to be lit.

1 Head through the gate towards LightFoot Village and Cape Claw (there's a switch on the ledge above the gate) and place a Fire Weed in the beacon. Have Tricky light the beacon with his "Flame" command.

2 The second beacon is located near the WarpStone on a small ledge above the water.

3 The third and final beacon is on top of the ledge overlooking the stream, between the Queen's temple and the ancient well.

Once all three beacons have been lit, the ThornTail who met Fox near the Arwing will rush over and reward the duo with the **Moon Pass Key**. The Key is just one of the items Fox should equip himself with before heading off to the Force Point Temple. Take this new possession and head to the ThornTail store to purchase the maps for Moon Mountain Pass and Volcano Force Point Temple. Bring along enough Scarabs to purchase the map to Krazoa Palace as well.

Drop down into the circular depression in the northeast corner of ThornTail Hollow and detonate a Bomb Spore near the crack in the wall. The path that opens leads to Moon Mountain Pass.

73

EN ROUTE TO VOLCANO FORCE POINT TEMPLE

MAP   To Moon Mountain Pass

TO
MOON
MOUNTAIN
PASS

COLLAPSE

TO
THORNTAIL
HOLLOW

74

Continue through the cave to the large circular area near the torches. The ground here is extremely brittle and will collapse under Fox's weight. Fortunately, an updraft of noxious gas is dense enough to keep Fox aloft. The bad news, of course, is that Fox can only breathe this poisonous air for so long—this is no time for sightseeing!

After the fall, turn to the left (the locator on the P.D.A map should point upwards) and float onto the narrow ledge. Straight ahead are two rising and falling rock spires. Wait for the tower on the right to bottom out and jump onto it. From there, jump to the second tower once it's below you. Lastly, jump into the opening in the cave on the other side of the gassy abyss and float back up to the surface. Don't worry about Tricky, he'll find another way around.

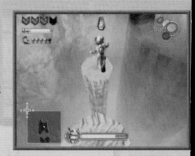

Continue on through the tunnel and into the wide canyon of Moon Mountain Pass. A pair of SharpClaw standing guard at the main gate atop the slope will do their best to thwart Fox's advances by hurling an endless barrage of barrels at him. Take cover behind the large rock outcroppings and in the nooks and crannies of the canyon walls. Try to collect the **Fuel Cell** located near the walls and make a final dash for the wooden gate.

Smash the SharpClaw Crates outside the gatehouse to regain some lost energy and use the Moon Pass Key to open the gate. Head through the gate and up the slope to the left to enter the gatehouse above. Grab the **Fuel Cell** from the wooden ledge and engage the pair of barrel-throwing SharpClaws inside.

The larger SharpClaw has a double-bladed battleaxe and can use it to deflect many of Fox's attacks. Defeating this variety of SharpClaw is a bit tougher. Fox will need to hold a defensive stance and wait until after the brute swings his axe before attacking. Even then, landing a clean hit isn't guaranteed. Continue counter-attacking until Fox can finally land a full combo-attack. This will send the SharpClaw to the floor. Waste no time in rushing over and initiating a second com-

bination. Hold Down on the ⚪ to perform Fox's twirling attack. Should the SharpClaw manage to interrupt the combo, step back and finish him off with the Fire Blaster. His lowly friend is not nearly the combatant he was and can be readily disposed of. Defeating these two SharpClaw will meet the requirements of the Life-Force Door blocking the entrance to the Force Point Temple.

MAP — To Volcano Force Point Temple

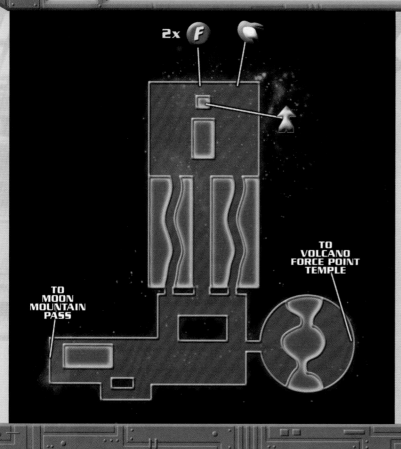

2x **F** 🦅

TO VOLCANO FORCE POINT TEMPLE

TO MOON MOUNTAIN PASS

Pass through the doorway where the Life-Force Door was located and wait for the three sliding platforms to extend out over the lava. Run and jump across the platforms in a zigzag pattern to reach the next room.

75

The path leading down to the large room up ahead is gated; Fox is going to need to take a more daring approach. Wait for the flame to dissipate in the vertical chute and then quickly jump down before the flame starts up again.

Dash past the flaming bats and use the Rocket Boost to reach the upper ledge along the back wall. This ledge contains three gates, each with valuable items behind it. For now, Fox can only open the gate on the far right. Flip the switch with the Staff and grab the **BafomDad** inside.

Jump down from the ledge and make the push up the conveyor belt in the center of the room. Perform multiple somersaults on the way up this ramp to avoid the barrels as best as possible. Leap across the lava in the following room and climb up the wall in the center to reach the true entrance to the Volcano Force Point Temple.

VOLCANO FORCE POINT TEMPLE PART 1

MAP VOLCANO FORCE POINT TEMPLE

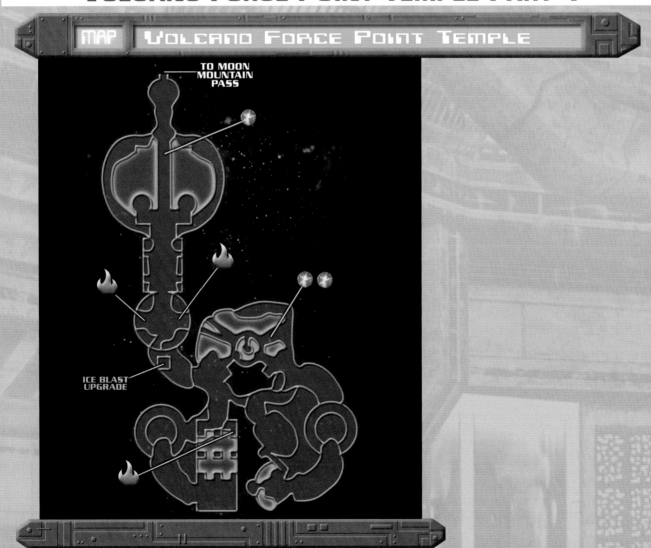

TO MOON MOUNTAIN PASS

ICE BLAST UPGRADE

Cross the bridge towards the large metal gate and place the SpellStone in the opening to continue on towards the Temple. Continue on towards the large door and approach the SharpClaw standing guard.

This particular SharpClaw is decked out in battle armor and even carries a heavy, iron shield. He is capable of blocking most of Fox's attacks with the shield and the double-bladed axe. Take a defensive stance and allow him to swing twice in a row. As soon as the axe passes by, press the (A) Button while holding Left on the (O) to strike away from the shield. Oftentimes these heavily armored SharpClaw soldiers will find a way to block the final blow in a combination attack. Fox should expect this and counter by starting the combination attack and then, instead of going for the fourth hit with the Staff, quickly switching to the Fire Blaster to finish him off!

LIGHTING OF THE ORBS

Fox may be surprised to see that the SpellStone cannot be used in the door to the Temple just yet. As the sign near the door reads, "only he who lights the orbs can pass". The orbs the sign refers to are the blue and green balls that flank the doorway.

1

1 Step back onto the bridge and aim the Fire Blaster towards the blue orb on the left, while keeping an eye on the changing colors of the flames in the cauldron. As soon as the flame turns blue, fire a blast through the edge of the flame and towards the orb.

2

2 Turn to the right and focus on the green orb just as you had the blue. Fire a shot from the Fire Blaster through the edge of the flame and at the orb as soon as the flame turns green.

77

FIRE-POWER — TIP

Even though the flames change from red to green to blue in a steady rhythm, it can still be difficult to get that shot off in time before it changes colors again. Fill up the Staff's power from the Magical Plant nearby and fire off a rapid succession of shots while the colors are changing.

Once the orbs are both glowing brightly, approach the doorway and take the SpellStone out from the inventory. The doors will open and Fox will finally have proven himself worthy of entering the Volcano Force Point Temple.

Fill up on health by smashing the SharpClaw Crates in the room and approach the Life-Force Door. According to the door, Fox must dispose of four bad guys to proceed. Although there are no enemies to be seen or heard from right now, four SharpClaw (two with shields) will appear as Fox returns towards the center of the room. Depending on how the battle flows, Fox may want to give Tricky his "Flame" command when squared off with the SharpClaw carrying shields—it makes the fight go much faster!

DIMMING OF THE KRAZOA FLAMES

As of now, Fox doesn't have the ability to extinguish flames. Nevertheless, with a little help from Tricky, that's all about to change!

1 Give Tricky his "Flame" command near each of the two red grates to extend the platforms above.

2 Climb the ladder and follow the upper walkway around through the previous room, past the flames, and then back to the doorway high on the wall in the circular room. Drop down the hole to receive the **Ice Blast** Staff upgrade.

3 remain on the upper ledge in the circular room and use the Ice Blast to extinguish each of the four red flames.

Once all four flames have been dimmed, the grate in the floor will slide out of view and a platform will rise up to carry Fox and Tricky deeper into the Temple.

VOLCANO FORCE POINT TEMPLE PART 3

The following corridors are certainly where the "Volcano" part of the Temple's name originates. Assign the Ice Blast to the 🔘 Button and get ready to use it douse the flaming bats as they attack.

Proceed to the large cavern in the center of the Temple. As Fox enters the room Peppy Hare will radio to Fox the story behind the Force Points. The mystical Krazoa placed two SpellStones in each of the Force Point Temples to hold back the internal powers of Dinosaur Planet so as to keep the planet from rifting apart. The current state of the planet is all because of General Scales. Fox is going to have to return all four SpellStones if Dinosaur Planet is to ever be whole again!

Approach the glowing panel directly in front of the door Fox just passed through. Use the SpellStone to gain further access into the Temple. Cross back the way from which Fox came and use the Ice Blast to extinguish the flame between the two doors. Walk across the grate and enter the corridor behind the other door. Step on the platform in the center of the room and ride it up to the final level in the Temple.

The large circular door at the end of the next corridor doesn't just open like the previous ones did. First Fox must douse the flames on the balcony in the circular room that the lift brought him too. Climb up the ladder and use the Ice Blast on each of the red flames to unbar the door.

Fox is getting very close to his ultimate destination. Enlist the help of Tricky and his "Flame" ability to defeat the three SharpClaw in the next room so as to remove the Life-Force Door blocking the way.

The next section of the Temple consists of a series of moving blocks floating between large fire jets. Hop onto the first moving block and wait for the flames to break. Once they do, quickly jump across the block and so forth to clear the lava pool. Once Fox makes it across, it becomes clear that this obstacle is just too much for Tricky—the lad is scared. Fortunately, each of the floating blocks can be brought to a halt right in the center of the pool with a careful shot from the Fire Blaster.

Shooting the panels moves the block to the center and freezes it there. Once Tricky is across the lava safely, have him "Flame" the red metal grate to the right of the door.

Venture down the windy path to the center of the Temple. There, Fox will be able to warp to the final room in the Volcano Force Point Temple where he can place the first Fire SpellStone in its ultimate resting place. Upon doing so, Fox will be magically warped back to the outer gates of the Temple. Turn your back to the Temple and set off back towards ThornTail Hollow.

NOTE — Fuel Cells Anyone?

On your way through the small fiery tomb between Volcano Force Point Temple and Moon Mountain Pass, be sure to Rocket Boost back up to the lengthy ledge in the central room. Now that Fox has the Ice Blaster he can extinguish the red flame to raise the gate and grab hold of the two **Fuel Cells** on the other side.

79

MOON MOUNTAIN PASS

A MESSAGE FROM THE KRAZOA PART 1

Just as Fox and Tricky begin crossing back through the canyon in Moon Mountain Pass, they are contacted by an unfamiliar voice: the voice of a girl in grave danger. Knowing that the twosome is confused by the foreign voice, a Krazoa Spirit makes an appearance on behalf of Krystal and explains the circumstances. The Krazoa Spirit charges Fox and Tricky with the task of completing each of the remaining five Krazoa Tests so as to eventually free the girl who calls out to them now. To point them in the right direction, the Krazoa Spirit opens a nearby door and hints at defeating the nearby creature to receive a MoonSeed.

The large creature in the crater is too much to handle right now; Fox must get a little stronger first. Enter the cave that the Krazoa Spirit opened up and move the stone in the room at the end to uncover another underground power-up location. Dive down into the hole to gain the **Ground Quake** Staff upgrade.

The clawed moon creature in the crater is covered in very thick scales and is not affected by Fox's Staff except for one spot—on his back. Collect enough Energy Gems from the nearby Magical Plants to fill the Staff's power meter and assign the Ground Quake to the Button for easy access. Walk up the creature and quickly perform the Ground Quake before he fires his first gaseous attack. This will cause it to spin around wildly inside the crater. Inch as close to him as possible and perform an overhead slash at the purple spot on his back when he spins around. Repeat this attack sequence one more time to finish him off and to get your first **MoonSeed**.

NOTE | MoonSeeds

MoonSeeds are a lot like Bomb Spore Plants. Both are planted in specific planting patches and both require a heat source to become useful. Look for planting areas near cliffs and have Tricky use his "Flame" skill to heat the seed. This will cause a lengthy vine to grow up the wall, thereby giving Fox a way to scale the wall. Fox can get more than enough MoonSeeds by defeating the crater creatures.

Plant the MoonSeed to the right of the tunnel and climb up to the ledge above. Up ahead lies another crater creature. Use the MoonSeed he drops to climb up to the rocky walkway to the north. Follow the path back towards the gatehouse to pick up an extra **BafomDad** and then return. Continue on through the canyon to the next crater creature and return to the site of the second one and plant the MoonSeed there.

Jump across to where the Bomb Spore Plant and the crater creature are and grab the **BafomDad** in the corner. Using the Ground Quake on this ledge will just cause the Bomb Spore Plant to erupt, which absorbs too much of the ripple to make the crater creature spin. Collect some Bomb Spores and hop across to the ledge with the bridge leading back to the left.

GEM COLLECTOR — TIP

The Ground Quake doesn't only serve as an excellent way to stun enemies, but also shakes Energy Gems loose from nearby Magical Plants. It might not sound like much, but the extra seconds saved during a heated battle can make a big difference.

Defeat the crater creature in the cave up ahead and then plant a Bomb Spore near the off-colored section of rock behind him. Blow through the cave wall to the outer area on the other side and continue down the path.

MOVING THE METEORITE

Just as Fox and Tricky begin to get accustomed to traveling through Moon Mountain Pass, a huge meteorite slams into the planet, causing an enormous explosion and sending the duo flying to the moon dirt. This oversized piece of space debris slid to a halt inside an important passage and must be moved in order for Fox and Tricky to reach the Krazoa Shrine.

The large boulder-like meteorite is resting atop a gas vent and although there is currently very little gas escaping underneath, that can be changed. Located just steps away from the meteorite are six other gas vents. If Fox can find something to plug some of these holes, the pressure will build up enough to unblock the important passage. Fortunately, there are three other (much smaller) meteorites that Fox can place in the holes.

DON'T CATER TO THE CRATER — TIP

Fox only needs one MoonSeed until much later in the level, so defeating each of the crater creatures isn't necessary. In fact, if there are any enemies in this area that warrant Fox's attention, it's the flying gargoyle-like beasts!

1 From where you enter via the cave, follow the eastern wall to a dry patch of dirt and give Tricky his "Find Secret" command. Pick up the small **Meteorite** and carry it towards the gas vents. Stand in one of the three vents furthest from the large meteorite and press the Ⓐ Button to lower the rock.

2 North of the gas vents is another dry patch of dirt that Tricky can dig in. Carry this second **Meteorite** back to the vents and drop it on one of the vents furthest from the blocked passage.

3 Head back to the east a few steps to find a flaming **Meteorite.** It will likely be a small chunk of the large one blocking the path! Use the Ice Blast to cool it off and carry it over to the vents and place it in the remaining vent furthest from the much larger meteorite.

Once all three Meteorites are placed in the correct positions, the pressure will build up underneath the larger meteorite and it will be lifted high off the ground. Be sure to climb up onto the ledge near where the second Meteorite was and grab the **Fuel Cell** and **BafomDad** before leaving this area.

A MESSAGE FROM THE KRAZOA PART 2

Sneak under the meteorite and plant a MoonSeed near the cliff. Have Tricky "Flame" the seed and climb up and over the cliff to the other side of the area. Descend the sloping path and plant another MoonSeed at the bottom. If Fox doesn't have any more MoonSeeds, he can acquire two of them from a pair of crater creatures to the north—there's also a couple of DumbleDang Pods there as well!

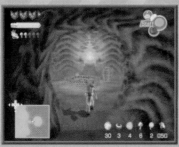

Ascend the zigzagging path to the south and plant one more MoonSeed near the ledge on the left. Fox can climb the vine to a cave containing a **Fuel Cell** and a **Cheat Token Well**. Jump down and continue to the south to the Krazoa Shrine Entrance Warp in the small building. Save your game progress and set off to the Krazoa Shrine.

Krazoa Shrine: Test of Combat

This Krazoa Shrine has slightly more complex obstacles leading to the Krazoa Spirit. But what's even more challenging is the Test of Combat. This is the most difficult Krazoa Test of all.

1 Jump into the water and swim past the two whirlpools to the other side. Use the Ice Blast to extinguish the flame and climb the wall to continue.

2 The next tank needs to be filled with water. Turn around and shoot the orange panel near the ceiling with the Fire Blaster to make this happen.

3 The room ahead contains a very narrow walkway that must be traversed while dodging the flames. Patience is the key to crossing this obstacle. Shoot the orange panel to open the gate.

Not So Fast! `TIP`

Don't rush up to the Spirit to begin the test until after Fox has smashed the SharpClaw Crates at the rear of the room. Make sure he's well-equipped going into this Test. This includes assigning the Fire Blaster to the ⬤ Button.

In order to complete the Test of Combat Fox must defeat ten SharpClaw within 3:30—and two of them are heavily protected with body armor and shields!

The most important step in this battle is to eliminate the larger, shield-carrying SharpClaws first. Since no damage is ever delivered to these tougher SharpClaw unless the fourth hit in the combination attack is landed, delivering a swift knockout can be difficult. Assume a defensive stance and allow them to take two swings at Fox. Quickly draw the Fire Blaster and begin backing away while firing a couple rounds at him. Direct hits with the Fire Blaster will not only inflict damage, but it opens him up to a follow-up attack.

KRAZOA SHRINE: TEST OF COMBAT

Once both of the larger SharpClaw are out of the picture, Fox can methodically sweep through the eight lesser SharpClaw. By relying strictly on the combination attack with the Staff, Fox can polish off these SharpClaw in less than seven seconds each! In other words, so long as there's at least a minute left on the timer after the two shield-carrying SharpClaw are defeated, you're in the clear!

NOTE: YOU DROPPED SOMETHING, BIG GUY!

Keep on the lookout for DumbleDang Pods and PukPuk Eggs as the SharpClaw (especially the larger ones) will periodically drop these rejuvenating goodies.

Once the Test of Combat is completed Fox will become the possessor of the second Krazoa Spirit and his eyes will turn purple to reflect the change. He will be automatically warped back to Moon Mountain Pass where Tricky awaits his safe return.

84

A MESSAGE FROM THE KRAZOA PART 3

As Fox exits the small building where the Entrance Warp was, the Krazoa Spirit that Krystal had freed appears. He explains to Fox that he must bring the Krazoa Spirit to Krazoa Palace without delay.

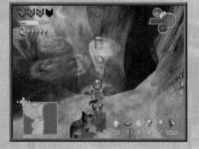

Descend the rocky bluffs and push northward through the canyon to the **Fuel Barrel** near the void. Toss the Fuel Barrel through the right-hand updraft so it will land gently on the rock platform. Jump across to it and then throw it clear across the area to the other rock platform. Finally, make your way onto the ledge near the crate and toss the Fuel Barrel against the rock wall. Head through the resulting tunnel and on to the updraft at the end. This will deliver Fox back to an area of Moon Mountain Pass much closer to the gatehouse.

Leave the Moon Mountain Pass area and head straight for the WarpStone in ThornTail Hollow. Once there, use the WarpStone to travel to Krazoa Palace.

RELEASING THE KRAZOA SPIRIT

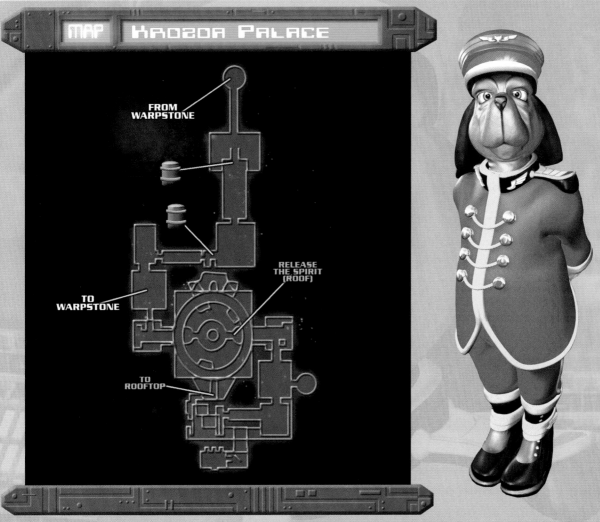

MAP KRAZOA PALACE

FROM WARPSTONE

TO WARPSTONE

RELEASE THE SPIRIT (ROOF)

TO ROOFTOP

Fox will arrive at Krazoa Palace alone, as the WarpStone cannot warp dinosaurs—not that Fox minds. Smash open the SharpClaw Crates near the ramp straight ahead to stock up on **FireFlies**.

Run up the ramp with the Staff in hand as four SharpClaw will materialize out of thin air. Defeat every last one of them to meet the requirements of the Life-Force Door. The next room is not only pitch-black but contains a mazelike walkway that leads to a large cracked wall.

Release a FireFly and grab the **Fuel Barrel** outside by the ramp. Carry the Fuel Barrel quickly into the darkened room and turn immediately to the right and climb the walkway. Make a left turn at the top of the ramp and proceed all the way to the next corner and turn to the right. In the middle of the room, along its eastern side, is a ramp leading down towards the cracked wall. Hurry along this path, turn left at the two torches, and a final right-hand turn at the bottom of the ramp. Quickly toss the Fuel Barrel at the wall before it self-detonates.

85

Enter the next room and use the Fire Blaster to shoot the orange panel high on the wall at the far end. This will cause the two fire jets in the center to start sliding back and forth across the room. Grab the **Fuel Barrel** on the right and carefully navigate a course through the two flames as they slide away from one another. The best way to do this is by following the left-hand flame towards the far end of the room and then quickly stepping over to the right once the flame on that side has past. Toss the Fuel Barrel at the wall to blast your way into the opulent room on the other side.

The next room features green and red orbs as well as a high-tech security gun…that happens to be behind an impenetrable force field. Stand back away from the large gun and aim the Fire Blaster at either of the orbs. Fox must once again shoot a beam through a flame and into the orb to light it. Remember, the flame must be the same color as the orb when the ray passes through it. Light both orbs to disable the force field and then open fire on the gun to destroy it.

Once the security gun is destroyed, Fox must return to the previous room to get another **Fuel Barrel**. Carry it back through the flames and place it on the black panel near the Krazoa Spirit statue. This will hold the door open for Fox to continue on through the Palace.

NOTE — Don't Warp!

The warp pad in the center of this room will send Fox back to the WarpStone in ThornTail Hollow. If Fox's eyes are still glowing purple, he's not ready to leave yet!

Board the octagonal platform across the next room to be lifted up to the tunnel above. Once in the room, turn to the left and approach the circular cathedral with the multiple levels of fans. Take to the air and glide back and forth across the fans to reach the highest (fourth) level in the Palace. And don't worry if Fox falls; he'll take a little damage but there are ladders for him to climb to escape the pit below.

Once safely on the uppermost tier, head to the southern end of the room and enter the alcove. The smaller fan tucked inside this narrow passage will float Fox to the roof of the Palace. Head up the ramp and allow Fox to meet Krystal.

After Fox is done drooling over the fox in the crystal, descend the ramp and approach the statue jutting out of the eastern side of the central structure. Press the Ⓐ Button while standing in the light to release the Krazoa Spirit. Once the Spirit is completely free, Fox will be sent back to ThornTail Hollow.

86

SPELLSTONE #2

FINDING THE SECOND SPELLSTONE

Fox returns to ThornTail Hollow to find Tricky waiting ever so patiently for him right by the foot of the WarpStone. The side trip to Krazoa Palace was a success, but they have to focus on the main task of saving Dinosaur Planet from General Scales. Peppy and Slippy will radio Fox through the Communicator alerting him that he needs to get to Cape Claw on the double!

THORNTAIL HOLLOW

The WarpStone may have seemed like a big, old, grump during the trip to Ice Mountain but he's ready to show his more generous side by offering Fox the **Medium Scarab Bag**. This satchel doubles Fox's Scarab carrying capacity from a paltry 50 to an impressive 100! Load up the bag back at the circle of stones and go shopping. Fox should purchase the **LightFoot Village Map**, **Cape Claw Map**, **CloudRunner Fortress Map**, and items that strike his fancy.

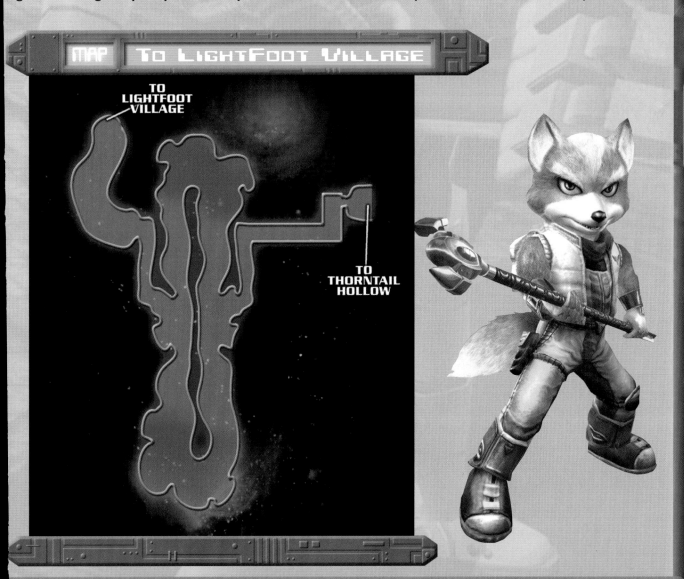

MAP — **To LightFoot Village**

TO LIGHTFOOT VILLAGE

TO THORNTAIL HOLLOW

Depart ThornTail Hollow through the open gate in the southwest corner of the map and follow the path to the clearing near the wooden spears. This area is a large circle, but because of the ledges leading in and out of the water to the north and south, it can only be traversed in a counter-clockwise direction. Make a right and jump down into the water. Swim around the bend and then turn to the right near the signpost to continue on towards LightFoot Village.

NOTE | SAVE YOUR SCARABS

It costs 60 Scarabs to open the gate to Cape Claw. Spend some time in ThornTail Hollow collecting at least 38 Scarabs to prevent having to backtrack. Fox will find 22 Scarabs under the rocks in LightFoot Village.

LIGHTFOOT VILLAGE

MAP | LIGHTFOOT VILLAGE

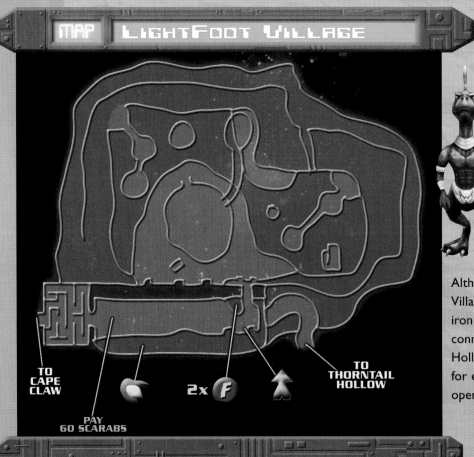

TO CAPE CLAW

PAY 60 SCARABS

2x **F**

TO THORNTAIL HOLLOW

Although the main part of the Village is sealed shut by a heavy iron gate, the lengthy courtyard connecting the paths to ThornTail Hollow and Cape Claw are open for exploration. This means they're open to SharpClaw as well!

88

Before Fox wanders too far, be sure and use the Rocket Boost to reach the top of the wall on the left. Follow the wall back towards the heavy gate and jump across to the ledge where the two **Fuel Cells** are located. Follow the ledges back around in the other direction to obtain an extra **BafomDad** and then jump down to the ground below.

There is a pair of SharpClaw patrolling the wooded path leading towards the entrance to Cape Claw. Eliminate them from this area with some repeat shots from the Fire Blaster and then approach the golden statue. Fox must deposit 60 Scarabs into the mouth of the statue in order to raise the enormous gate blocking the path to Cape Claw. Although there are numerous Scarabs under the boulders in this area, Fox may have to return to ThornTail Hollow to meet the toll.

The maze leading out of LightFoot Village can be easily navigated by looking at Fox's P.D.A, but care must be given to avoid the fox-eating plants that cling to the walls. Approach each corner slowly as the plants will strike out with their long tendrils. Fox can either beat the tendrils back with his Staff or somersault past them.

Descend the ladder into the extremely deep well below. There are numerous ladders, ledges, and Rocket Boost Pads here in the well, but where Fox really needs to go is on the uppermost ledge, across from where he enters. Descend one extra ladder and cross the walkway over to the ladder to the south and climb up to enter Cape Claw. Before climbing up, grab the three Fuel Cells at the bottom of the well.

ALL YOU CAN EAT! ⬛ TIP

There aren't any hidden secrets at the bottom of the well, but there is a bounty of GrubTubs for Tricky. If Fox is running low on GrubTubs, there's no better place to stock up than at the bottom of the well.

CAPE CLAW

FREEING QUEEN CLOUDRUNNER PART 1

No wonder the ShopKeeper says he wants to move to Cape Claw, this place is beautiful! Situated on a quiet bay, Cape Claw has everything from cascading waterfalls to mountain views to, er, SharpClaw—lots and lots of ugly SharpClaw. Ok, so maybe this place isn't so picturesque after all!

Descend the path past the first axe-wielding beast and follow the trail southward towards the large waterfall. Use the Fire Blaster to hit the orange panel to extend the bridge across the gap. Drop off the bridge onto the rock outcropping directly below to grab the **Fuel Cell** and then swim to the docks by the cliff.

Lead Fox onto the beach where he will encounter numerous sand-dwelling monsters. These beasts will sooner disappear below ground than stick around to fight, but if Fox does manage to slay one, he'll be rewarded with an Energy Gem. Lift the rock on the northern end of the beach and collect the Scarabs underneath and then head up the walkway in the middle of the bay.

The BribeClaw standing guard over the imprisoned HighTop doesn't like the looks of Fox but he's willing to let him talk to the HighTop in exchange for 25 Scarabs. Pay the bribe and approach the HighTop. Or, if you want to skip the bribe, use the Boost Pad behind and below the BribeClaw. Members of the HighTop Tribe are very docile creatures and this one is no exception. He'll make Fox an offer he and Tricky can't refuse: find his four gold bars and he'll help them out with their quest.

THE HIGHTOP'S LOST GOLD

Each of the four gold bars have buried somewhere in the sand so it's going to be up to Tricky to dig them up. Locate each of the dirt patches and give Tricky the "Find Secret" command.

1 The first **Gold Bar** is in the northeast corner of the large beach.

2 Swim across to the western beach and have Tricky dig up the **Gold Bar** between the two trees while Fox defends the pair against the SharpClaw.

3 Have Tricky burn through the briers near #2 and go through the tunnel to the northwestern corner. Take care of the two enormous SharpClaw while Tricky digs up the **Gold Bar** in the puddle.

4 The final **Gold Bar** is buried under the SharpClaw Crate near the jail cell.

Once all of the treasure is found, return to the HighTop and hand it over to him. To keep his end of the deal, the HighTop will rise up on his hind legs and slam his weight down to the ground in such a thunderous force that a ladder in the southwest corner of the area will fall. Fox now has a way to reach the switch on the wall!

FREEING QUEEN CLOUDRUNNER PART 2

Swim across to the large shrine in the south end of Cape Claw and run up the ramp and to the right. Use the Staff to flip the switch on the platform above the ladder. Although this doesn't open the doors to the CloudRunner's cell, it does open up the gates to a secret corridor directly above her.

Although the room seems empty at first, as soon as Fox breaks for the door he will find himself sealed in with a poisonous gas leaking in from four grates. The four blocks that were in the center of the room have slid to the corners and if Fox wants to ever leave this room, he's got to push them back into place before the gas does him in.

Quickly run to the block nearest Fox and press the Ⓐ Button while standing next to it to grab hold. Use the ⚪ to slide/push/pull the block over the grate. Although pushing the block is fastest, it's very hard to line up with the grate. For this reason, we recommend grabbing the block by the side and pulling it laterally to line it up with the grate, and then pushing it home. The faster the grates get blocked up, the more fresh air Fox will have available. In an emergency, Fox can stand on the block in the corner to get some air back.

NO TIME FOR FIGHTING
TIP

Avoid pushing the Ⓐ Button while running up to the blocks as this will cause Fox to draw his Staff and begin swinging it, which wastes considerable time. Instead, come to a halt next to the block before pushing that Ⓐ Button. This is Fox's cue to grab the block instead.

91

With the puzzle completed, and the bars to the jail cell lowered, Fox is ready to meet up with the Queen of the CloudRunners Tribe. Tricky is not nearly as excited as the EarthWalkers and CloudRunners are political adversaries. Nevertheless, if General Scales has made it to CloudRunner Fortress, then that's where Fox must go too!

Head back to the Arwing in ThornTail Hollow and set course for CloudRunner Fortress! Tricky will wait in the Hollow.

Shoo, shoo! Go away, CloudRunner, get away!

SPACE TRAVEL

DESTINATION: CLOUDRUNNER FORTRESS

The ripping of CloudRunner Fortress from the surface of Dinosaur Planet has resulted in a large belt of ruins and asteroids which Fox must pilot the Arwing through.

Fuel Cells Needed: 10

Gold Rings: 5 of 10

Time: 1:00

1 Fly to the right-hand side of the first rock island as soon as it appears. The first Gold Ring is in the rock arches.

2 Aim straight for the center of the second island. The next Gold Ring is directly in the center of the cracks in the ancient building atop the island.

3 Head to the left after exiting the tunnel on the second island. The third gold ring will be rising and falling so anticipate its movement and adjust for it.

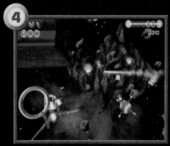

4 Fly through the ruins ahead and then dart to the left. The fourth Gold Ring is hovering just below the floating platform before the minefield.

5 The next Gold Ring is drifting back and forth across the plains on the stony island ahead. Shoot out the "X" inside it and then anticipate its position and zip through it.

CloudRunner Fortress

Helping the Queen Part 1

MAP   CloudRunner Fortress

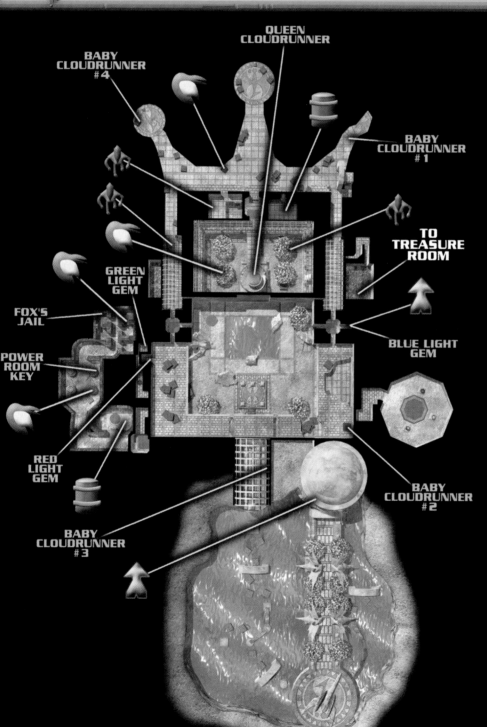

QUEEN CLOUDRUNNER

BABY CLOUDRUNNER #4

BABY CLOUDRUNNER #1

TO TREASURE ROOM

GREEN LIGHT GEM

FOX'S JAIL

BLUE LIGHT GEM

POWER ROOM KEY

RED LIGHT GEM

BABY CLOUDRUNNER #2

BABY CLOUDRUNNER #3

The SharpClaw have overrun the Fortress and locked the gate. Unlike the Queen CloudRunner, Fox can't simply fly over the walls, so he's going to have to find another way inside. Battle past the two SharpClaw and descend the ladder on the right to the lake below. Swim across to the platform to the north.

In order to get the switch controlling the main gates to appear, Fox must race around the lake in under thirty seconds. Step on the large panel to start the clock and immediately start running. Fox will automatically jump the proper distance from crate to crate, so the player just has to steer him in the right direction. Ignore any diversions off to the side—Fox has plenty of time to collect Energy Gems later—and try to keep a steady pace. The only time it pays to slow down and take it easy is when walking across the narrow wall.

Once Fox successfully passes through all three magical arches, an orange panel will appear above the gates to the Fortress. Climb the ladder back to the tree-lined walkway above and shoot this panel with the Fire Blaster to enter.

Climb the spiraling walkway while dodging the lasers of the sentry drones hovering in the air. The drones can only be stunned with the Fire Blaster, so it is best to accept the one block of damage they might deliver and just continue running. Once at the very top of the tower, descend the ladder beside the gated hallway. Walk counter-clockwise along this ledge to the switch on the far wall. Return the way you came and go through the newly opened doorway.

While Fox was busy trying to get into the Fortress, General Scales was able to capture the Queen. Thankfully, Fox gets there in time to interrupt the evil plans the General had for the Queen, or so he thought. Three drones immediately swarm Fox and knock him unconscious while the Queen is taken away.

BREAKING OUT OF THE SLAMMER

Fox comes to in a dreary prison cell and notices right away that his Staff has been stolen. He's got to find a way out of here—wherever "here" is.

Approach the gray block in the wall by the door and push it through to the next cell. Luckily, the next cell has no prisoner and the door has been left open. Just as Fox begins his escape, Slippy radios him with a plan. He tells Fox that he has made a SharpClaw Disguise and can drop it off, provided Fox find a way of opening up part of the ceiling somewhere.

Although the adjoining cells contain SharpClaw crates, Fox has no way to smash them open. That being the case, head up the path to the room where a pair of CloudRunners is being held. Sneak quietly around the right-hand side of the room to avoid the sleeping guard, and whatever you do, don't splash in any puddles!

NOTE | No Staff For You!

Even though the Staff is just sitting out in the open on the guard's desk, Fox can't just run up and take it. Should Fox try to take it back the guard will wake up and call for backup. This, of course, will lead to him being thrown back in the slammer.

Exit the room via the corridor near the guard and descend the ladder off to the left. There, Fox will find a **Fuel Barrel**, a fan, and a panel in the floor. Carry the Fuel Barrel over to the fan and set it down. Now stand on the panel to turn on the fan and watch and behold as the Fuel Barrel's timer goes off and it blows a hole in the ceiling of the cave! Slippy will send Fox the **SharpClaw Disguise**.

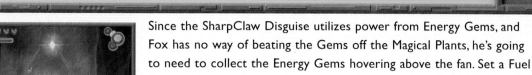

Diamonds in the Sky | TIP

Since the SharpClaw Disguise utilizes power from Energy Gems, and Fox has no way of beating the Gems off the Magical Plants, he's going to need to collect the Energy Gems hovering above the fan. Set a Fuel Barrel down on the panel to turn on the fan and then ride the winds to the Energy Gems above.

Don the SharpClaw Disguise and approach the slumbering guard at the desk. He'll leave Fox to watch over the Staff and the prisoners while he goes on break. Take back the Staff and use it to flip the four switches near the caged CloudRunners. Fox will then learn that the power has been shut off and the Wind Lifts must be restarted if he's to ever find the SpellStone. He provides Fox with the **Power Room Key** to help him accomplish his goal. Finish looting the room (don't miss the **BafomDad** inside the SharpClaw Crate) and then head up the corridor after the CloudRunner.

95

NOTE | For SharpClaw Only

In order for Fox to smash open the smaller crate in the room, he's going to have to use the SharpClaw Disguise. These boxes can only be picked up by a SharpClaw, as they're too heavy for a mere fox. Fox will soon encounter Fuel Barrels with the same property.

RESTORING THE POWER

Shoot the orange panel near the door with the Fire Blaster to open it, and continue on. The switch on the wall by the CloudRunner controls the nearby Wind Lift, but since the power is currently off, little can be done with it.

Climb to the top of the tower on the other side of the door, but be careful to avoid the drones. Watch for their searchlights to revolve past Fox's location and then quickly climb to the walkway above. There are three sections of brick wall for Fox to climb before he reaches the hall leading to the courtyard. Smash the Crates for the PukPuk Eggs to refill his health and step around the rubble and into the clearing.

The CloudRunner Tribe prides themselves on their tranquil surroundings, and it shows in their decorative courtyards and terraces. Unfortunately, the rifting apart of Dinosaur Planet has left their main courtyard littered with rubble and obstacles. In order to restore the power to the Fortress, Fox must race against the clock to locate various gems. It's important to do some preliminary reconnaissance to ensure that the clock doesn't win.

Loop around the rubble and approach the northern wall of the courtyard, just to the east of where Fox entered. Climb onto the large crate and smash the SharpClaw Crate resting atop it. Flip the switch behind it to lower the nearby ladder. Climb the ladder and use the Ice Blast to extinguish the flames in the floor of the corridor above.

Cross the yard to the south and approach the hall leading away from the pool. Use the Ice Blast to douse these flames as well.

Fox is now ready to unlock the room with the generator in it. Head to the southwest corner of the courtyard and use the Power Room Key to unlock the door. Inside, Fox will find three obelisks each with a slot for a missing Light Gem. In order to restore the power, Fox must return all three Gems. The three pedestals on the large platform near the pool are each linked to a gate somewhere in the area. Fox must push against these pedestals to raise their corresponding gate and then rush off to unlock the lockbox behind the gate before it lowers. One of the Light Gems can be found in each of these lockboxes.

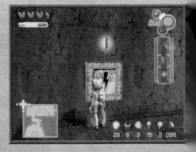

Into Thin Air | TIP

If you're planning on collecting all three Light Gems and returning them at once, don't do it. The Generator Room is filled with a poisonous gas and Fox has to place all three gems.

1 Push against the left-hand pedestal and run counter-clockwise around the plat-form to reach the ladder lowered earlier. Rush through the corridor to the lockbox and use the Staff to open it to gain the **Green Light Gem**.

2 Press against the middle pedestal to raise a gate on the upper walkway. Return back towards the Generator Room and scamper up the large stack of crates to reach the second level. Dash past the SharpClaw patrolling the area and into the alcove to recover the **Red Light Gem**.

3 Push the right-hand pedestal's panel in to open the gate high on the wall in the southeastern hall. Use the Rocket Boost to leap up to the ledge and claim the **Blue Light Gem**.

Once the third Light Gem is in place, the power will automatically come up and the Wind Lifts will begin functioning. In fact, those pesky sentry drones will all be blown right out of the Fortress!

HELPING THE QUEEN PART 2

After all of this, Fox still hasn't found Queen CloudRunner! Exit the Generator Room and cross the yard to the north. Enter the hall in the northeast corner and ride the Wind Lift upwards. From here, enter the hall to the right where the three SharpClaw are on patrol.

A gate will slam down behind Fox when he enters this hall and the only way out is to don the SharpClaw Disguise. Grab the Ice Blast and use it to put each of the baddies on ice and quickly perform an overhead strike with the Staff to destroy them

with one shot! Once they're gone, put on the outfit and step onto the panel by the gate leading outside.

There are many SharpClaw milling about in this area, and each of them must be destroyed in order to unlock the Life-Force Door. Use the freeze-and-slash tech-nique with the Ice Blast to quickly dispose of the five SharpClaw. Climb onto the stack of crates on the middle peninsula and leap back towards the Fortress to claim the **BafomDad**.

97

Put on the SharpClaw Disguise once again and use it to pick up the **Fuel Barrel** in the room behind the Life-Force Door. Carry the explosives to the room north of the heavy gate and set it down on the metal plate. Climb the ladder to the ledge above and step onto the SharpClaw Pad to have the magnetic lift bring the Fuel Barrel up to the second floor. Grab the Fuel Barrel and carry it out onto the balcony and throw it at the wooden barricade between the two lanterns.

With the blockade blown to smithereens, Fox can now pass through the central corridor to the next courtyard. When trying to do this, however, the wooden grate in the floor breaks, dropping Fox down to the corridor below. Fox can still enter the courtyard, but now he has to contend with a small contingent of SharpClaw.

Once the SharpClaw are beaten into submission, head to the far right-hand corner to find a SharpClaw Pad. Stand on the Pad while wearing the SharpClaw Disguise to lower a ladder. Climb the ladder and follow the walkway back to the same corner where the Pad is to find a switch. This is one of two switches that must be flipped to open the gate blocking the lower level corridor.

Approach the large cage in the center and talk to the jailed Queen. She'll inform Fox that the support below the cage feels unstable. Perhaps he can break it? Head around the left side of her cage and jump onto the two large crates. From there, jump to the ledge and flip the second switch. Now Fox has a way of bringing a Fuel Barrel into this area!

Return to the outer part of the Fortress and use the SharpClaw Disguise to grab another **Fuel Barrel**. Enter the corridor where the gate was and float the Fuel Barrel through the updraft to the other side. Jump across and use the Fuel Barrel to detonate the support beam for the Queen's cage. Now that the Queen is free, she and Fox can finally come up with a plan on finding the SpellStone!

SAVE THE CHILDREN!

The Queen is thankful for Fox rescuing her, but she can't help but be concerned over her four children. Her kids flew off when General Scales captured her and she now fears for their lives. The Queen gives Fox the **CloudRunner Flute** and asks him to use it to lead her four children back home to safety.

NOTE | ONE BABY AT A TIME

The CloudRunner's babies must be rescued in the order in which the cutscenes show them being harassed. A meter will appear showing how long it is before the baby last shown finally succumbs to the SharpClaw. Fox must eliminate the threat and then blow the CloudRunner Flute to let the baby know that it's time to fly home.

1 The first **baby CloudRunner** is on the southeastern peninsula outside the courtyard. Defeat the SharpClaw and blow the CloudRunner Flute while standing on the crate below the one the baby is on.

2 Head west along the side of the Fortress and shoot the orange panel to open the gate leading to the earlier courtyard. Float across the gap and continue straight ahead towards the next **baby CloudRunner**. Blow the Flute near the crate after defeating the two SharpClaw.

3 The third baby CloudRunner is the trickiest of all to locate. From #2, jump down to the courtyard grass below and weave through the rubble west of the ramp leading up to the three pedestals used earlier. Enter the tunnel on the left and descend the ladder to the right. Smash the SharpClaw crate to reveal a Rocket Boost Pad. Rocket up to the rooftop and quickly dispose of the three SharpClaw in the grass to the left to save the third **baby CloudRunner**.

4 The fourth and final **baby CloudRunner** is on the northwestern peninsula outside of the Fortress. Head back the way you came (you may have to flip the switch on the Wind Lift to ride it upwards) and take on the four SharpClaw with the Ice Blast.

Now that all four of the Queen's children have been returned safely, Fox can claim his reward. The Queen holds up her end of the bargain and opens the door to the Treasure Room. She believes it's where General Scales hid the SpellStone.

RAIDING THE TREASURE ROOM

The CloudRunner may have opened the door leading down into the Treasure Room, but Fox is going to need some hefty firepower to break into the room where the SpellStone is being held. Before anything else, Fox must perform some brief reconnaissance work.

Say farewell to the Queen and head back outside to the large exterior terrace. Head south towards the arch and descend the ladder to the windy path leading to the Treasure Room. Follow the amber glow into the tomb below the Fortress and collect the **Fire Flies** on the ledge beyond the SharpClaw. Scout out the area ahead to make sure the Wind Lift is blowing upward and then ride it back up to the outer area.

Don the SharpClaw Disguise and pick up the **Fuel Barrel** one final time. Slowly approach the corridor leading back towards the Queen CloudRunner and gently toss the Fuel Barrel into the windy currents. If done correctly, the Fuel Barrel will bounce around a little, but will remain aloft.

Quickly descend back to the tomb towards the switch controlling the Wind Lift. Take off the SharpClaw Disguise and use the Staff to set the Wind Lift to the "down" position to lower the Fuel Barrel. Let a FireFly loose, put on the SharpClaw Disguise, and grab the Barrel once again.

Enter the pitch-black room at the end of the tunnel and head around the fallen column. Look for the light shining through a crack in the wall to the north and toss the Fuel Barrel at it to gain access to the ladder leading down into the underground area.

Not So Fast!   TIP

Don't miss out on the Magical Plant and the **BafomDad** on the ledge inside the darkened room. They're located near the tunnel leading back to the Wind Lift.

THE RACE FOR THE SPELLSTONE

MAP   CloudRunner Lower

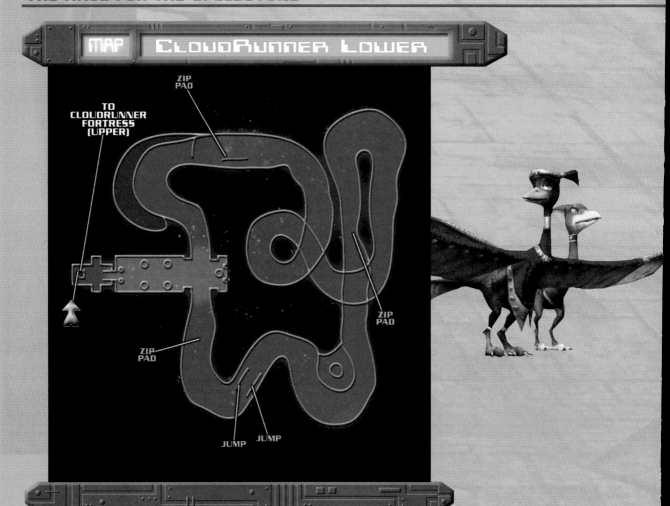

Fox will slip off the ladder and freefall down into an underground cave system below. Brush yourself off and head through either doorway to meet up with General Scales and his army of SharpClaw! Not about to let Fox get another SpellStone, Scales has three of his best soldiers race off into the caves with it on SharpClaw Racers. And with a press of a button, the General disappears into thin air. Fox doesn't have any time to waste and quickly mounts the third SharpClaw Racer and races off after the SharpClaw.

Unlike the race at Ice Mountain, this one takes place on a circuitous course and isn't so much a race to the finish, but a race to the death! In order to get his hands on the second SpellStone, Fox must put the SharpClaw and their SharpClaw Racers out of commission. Each of the hover bikes can only take so much damage before finally erupting into a ball of flame. In order to achieve this, Fox must not only catch up to the SharpClaw, but he must then proceed to ram them into the walls of the cave until their metallic steed blows apart.

This is not as simple as it sounds. As Fox found out during his snowbound journey at Ice Mountain, the SharpClaw love to drop numerous mines behind them as they go. This is in addition to the many flames, rocks, and falling pieces of debris that Fox must already steer clear of.

Fox's racer has a power meter that directly correlates to the racer's maximum speed. Thankfully, there are large yellow "zip pads" that, when driven over, restore power back to the racer and increase its overall speed.

Continue racing around the track, lap after lap until finally all three of the SharpClaw Racers have been destroyed and the **Water SpellStone** is in your grasp. The following tips should help:

No Brakes!

Don't worry about having to slow down, just keep the (A) Button pressed the entire time. The SharpClaw Racer can take every turn at maximum speed.

AVOID THE MINES

When closing in on a SharpClaw watch his movements closely. The SharpClaw will turn around and sneer at Fox right before dropping a mine. Swing alongside him to avoid hitting it.

DEATH FROM ABOVE

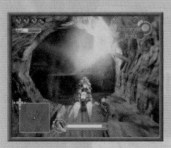

The biggest way to dish out punishment to the SharpClaw without taking any yourself is to hit the jumps on the side of the track and land on top of them. It's tough to get the timing down, but few attacks are more satisfying.

EVERY ZIP COUNTS

This should go without saying, but try to steer the bike across each and every zip pad so as to keep the racer at its top end speed. Consult the map for the locations of the three zip pads.

READY, SET, BRAKE!

There is one good time to apply the brakes, and it's when there's a SharpClaw on your tail. This is a particularly good strategy to employ when there's only one SharpClaw left and your racer is too fast to stay behind him.

The CloudRunners are indebted to Fox for fending off General Scales and look forward to rebuilding their Fortress. The Queen wishes Fox luck in returning the SpellStone to the Ocean Force Point Temple and sends him off with a royal tribute. Fox has earned a fifth Heart.

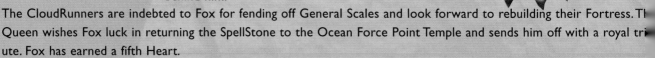

NOTE   FLYING HOME

The flight back to Dinosaur Planet is always the same: no Fuel Cells are consumed and the Arwing only needs to be flown through 1 Gold Ring to open the Force Field. See the first *ThornTail Hollow* chapter for tips on Gold Ring location.

DELIVERING THE SECOND SPELLSTONE

As soon as Fox steps out of the Arwing, Tricky is there to greet and congratulate him. Boy, did the little tike ever miss his buddy Fox! Play catch with him for a moment and stock up on supplies at the ThornTail Store. Be sure to purchase the **Ocean Force Point Temple Map.** When properly outfitted, head off for Cape Claw.

CAPE CLAW

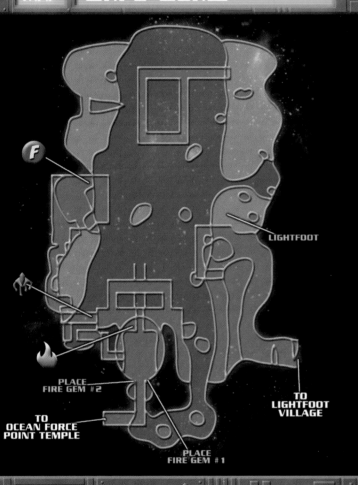

Follow the path around to the front of the temple entrance along the south end of the Cape and climb the ladder to the upper walkway. Put on the SharpClaw Disguise and step on the SharpClaw Pad to open the door.

Swim across to the pedestal on the left and stand atop the red panel to cause a second pedestal to rise above the water's surface. Make Tricky "Stay" on the panel while Fox uses the raised pedestal to flip the switch on the wall above the ledge. This will shut off the waterfall outside, thereby allowing Fox to swim into the cave behind it.

Head back outside, dive into the water, and swim through the tunnel that the waterfall was obscuring. Continue to fight against the current until reaching the narrow ledge at the end of the cave.

Drop down into the room below and watch as a flame kicks up in front of the Krazoa statue. Use the Ice Blast to extinguish the flame and take the **Fire Gem** mounted in the statue's mouth. This will trigger a massive flooding of the room. Swim back outside through the opening opposite the statue.

Go up the ramp and enter the room directly above the one Fox was just in. On the back wall are two more Krazoa Statues. Place the Fire Gem in the statue on the left and then exit the room.

Travel to the eastern side of the Cape and descend the wooden walkway to the beaches. There, Fox will encounter a LightFoot Tribe member trying to beat back two SharpClaw. Rush to the LightFoot's assistance to learn a little about his thieving ways. Shortly after, a SharpClaw across the bay will begin lobbing cannonballs at the LightFoot in hopes of getting a gem back. The LightFoot becomes scared and tosses the second **Fire Gem** to Fox.

Return to the central room "behind the ancient" as the HighTop would say and place the second Fire Gem in the mouth of the statue to the right. Opposite this statue is a pedestal with a switch alongside it, controlling its movements. Have Tricky "Stay" on top of the pedestal while Fox flips the switch to raise it into the air. Once it is at its maximum height, give Tricky his "Flame" command. Once Tricky removes the briars and the sunlight is able to wash over the second Fire Gem, the door to the Ocean Force Point Temple will open.

Head through the doorway and follow the hall to the next room. A gate currently blocks the route to Ocean Force Point Temple; Fox has one more puzzle to solve to gain access to the Temple. Cross the room to the gate and use the Fire Blaster and shoot the orange panel over the doorway Fox entered the room through. This will cause a massive flood in the room and Fox will float up to the upper balcony. Enter the

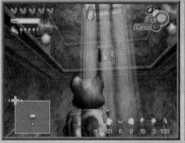

corridor and have Tricky burn the briars in the middle of the passage. Push the concrete block down into the water and then shoot the panel once again to turn it from green back to orange. Slide the block onto the black panel in the floor of the room to open the gate.

OCEAN FORCE POINT TEMPLE PART 1

Cross the sandy area towards the Temple's true entrance and climb the ladders on the right to the upper landing. A well-armed SharpClaw will materialize in hopes of bringing Fox's progress to a halt, but even he can be frozen with the Ice Blast and destroyed with a single strike of the Staff. Place the SpellStone over the glowing pane to open the gate. Descend the winding passage to the large room below.

ELECTRIC FLOOR PUZZLE

The hall leading south towards the SharpClaw is covered in a high-voltage current that will not only knock Fox on his backside, but will sizzle a few hairs on his head too! There is a pattern to which one can safely walk across this booby-trapped floor, but it requires teamwork to pull off.

Head up the ramp in the center of the room and stand atop the panel to light the grid on the wall. Have Tricky take Fox's place on the panel to keep the lights on and guide Fox over towards the electrified floor.

The six lights on the wall represent the path one must follow traverse the electric floor. The squares that are lit on the wall essentially provide a map as to which ones are safe to walk across on the floor. Once a "safe" square is stepped on, the entire row will be powered-down and become safe for travel. The thing to remember is that the grid on the wall is *not* a mirror image of the one on the floor.

Instead, a block that is "third from the left" on the wall corresponds to the block "third from the left" when turned around and facing the electric floor.

Take the crossing of the electric floor one block at a time and always turn around double-check which square to step on next. The Hi-Def Display goggles can really come in handy for the last couple rows when Fox is furthest from the grid. Once the electric floor is disabled, whistle for Tricky and head down the hall to defeat the SharpClaw.

SHARPCLAW GET HUNGRY TOO! TIP

Put on the SharpClaw Disguise and smash the miniature SharpClaw-only crates lying around near the grid. The PukPuk Eggs and DumbleDang Pods will be especially beneficial if Fox took a lot of damage from the electric floor.

105

OCEAN FORCE POINT TEMPLE PART 2

Take out the SharpClaw with the freeze-n-slash method and jump into the water on the left. Dodge the two turtle-like creatures in the water and swim across to the small platform along the northern wall. From there, jump onto the narrow elevated paths that lead upwards from the center. Walk along each path to the three switches on the wall and use the Staff to flip each of them. There are Fuel Cells next to the switch at the end of the path.

CRAFTY TURTLES TIP

The creatures swimming in the water are a lot like turtles in that their shell is practically indestructible. If low on health, instead of risking injury from them while swimming, wait for their heads to rise up out of the shell and then shoot them with the Fire Blaster

Now that the water flowing out of the drainpipe has been stopped, Fox can swim down the corridor in the southeast corner of the room. Climb the rock wall up to the platform above and shoot a beam from the Fire Blaster through the flame and into the orb on the pedestal when the two are the both green. This will unlock the warp and allow Fox to reach the lower area of Ocean Force Point Temple. Grab the two Fuel Cells next to the flame.

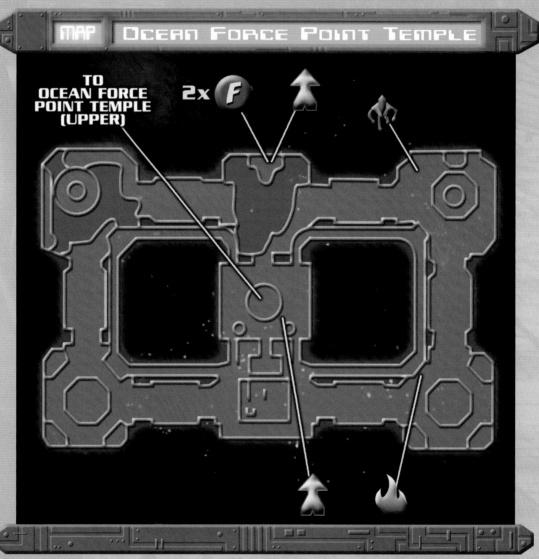

MAP **OCEAN FORCE POINT TEMPLE**

TO
OCEAN FORCE
POINT TEMPLE
(UPPER)

2x ⒡

Two enormous, iron-plated SharpClaw ambush Fox as soon as he appears in the lower area of the Temple. Quickly Ice Blast one of them while letting Tricky take of the other with his "Flame" command. The doors at the north end of the room will open when Fox approaches them. Enter the next room to gain some extra Energy Gems and to use the Rocket Boost to find the two **Fuel Cells** on the upper ledge.

NORTHEAST ROOM PUZZLE

Swim across to the platform along the northern wall and flip the switch to lower the water. Jump down and flip the switch across the room to open the southern door. Now for the tricky part: reaching the switch that controls the water level.

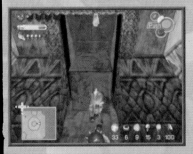

Don the SharpClaw Disguise once again and step on the SharpClaw Pad to raise the door on the eastern side of the central tower. Grab hold of the block that's revealed and push it into the slot in the south side of the tower and climb onto it. Now Fox can reach the switch that raises the water. Swim across to the south exit and proceed to the next room.

SOUTHEAST ROOM PUZZLE

Locate the grate in the corner and have Tricky blow his fire into it to start the puzzle in this room. Fox has 3:30 to extinguish the four yellow flames in the center of the room and the only way it can be done is by having the Krazoa statues near the ceiling blow the flames out. Each of the statues has an orange panel below it. When the Fire Blaster shoots this panel, the statue will bend forward and blow an icy cold air downward.

Complicating things is the fact that the four yellow flames are on a revolving platform that only pauses momentarily every 1/4 turn. Because of this, Fox must anticipate when the flame will be in the right position and have the Krazoa statue already bending down to meet the flame with its cold air. A good place to stand to be able to hit all four panels is on either of the elevated platforms. Not only does this provide a birds-eye-view of the room, but there's a Magical Plant on each of the platforms as well!

NOTE | NO TWO SIDES ARE ALIKE

The placement of the flames and the shape of the pedestal prohibit each flame from matching up perfectly with each Krazoa statue. Instead, the flames are paired with the one diagonally across from it, and the corresponding Krazoa statue. This means that the same Krazoa statue cannot be used to blow out two flames in a row, as the second flame will pass by without pausing underneath it.

107

SOUTH CENTRAL ROOM PUZZLE

This room features a puzzle in the strictest sense of the word. The large pit in the center of the room has several gray walls and a floating crate with orange panels all around it. The crate must be guided through the puzzle towards the green and red flames with blasts from the Fire Blaster. Shoot an orange panel to send the crate floating across the pit in the opposite direction. The catch to this

is that the crate will reset back at its initial location if it comes into contact with the sides of the pit. In other words, the crate must only come into contact with the various gray walls.

The following directions detail the directions in which the crate must be "pushed" to reach the goal:

1:	East	4:	South
2:	North	5:	East
3:	West	6:	North

Once the puzzle is completed, the Rocket Boost Pad in the central room will become active. Rush back to the center room and Rocket up to the balcony above.

OCEAN FORCE POINT TEMPLE

There's only way to go once Fox is on the narrow balcony. Follow the path counter-clockwise to the northeast room and fire a shot from the Fire Blaster through the flame and into the orb in the upper corner. The orb changes colors with the flame, so both are always the same color.

Walk across the bridge that is extended to access the warp pad. Fox will be warped away to the ultimate Force Point location—the room where the SpellStones are placed. Set the SpellStone in the center pedestal to complete the second phase of the quest.

Fox will automatically be transported back on the sands outside the Temple. Start back towards ThornTail Hollow.

LIGHTFOOT VILLAGE

A TRIBAL TRAP

MAP   LIGHTFOOT VILLAGE

TO KRAZNA SHRINE

TOTEM #3

F

CHIEF LIGHTFOOT'S HUT

SQUARE BLOCK CARVING

LIGHTFOOT FAMILY #3

F

TOTEM #1

BABLES IN THE FOREST

TRIANGLE BLOCK CARVING

BABLES UNDERGROUND

CHEAT TOKEN WELL

BABLES IN TREES

LIGHTFOOT FAMILY #1

TO CAPE CLAW

TOTEM #4

CIRCLE BLOCK CARVING

TOTEM #2

TO THORNTAIL HOLLOW

LIGHTFOOT FAMILY #2

Just as Fox and Tricky begin making their way across the outer area of LightFoot Village, Fox gets swarmed by a mob of angry LightFoot Tribe members. When he comes to, he finds himself tied to a totem pole. Yep, Fox is in deep water!

That's the steenking beast that took my treasure

Fortunately for Fox, a CloudRunner spotted the whole scene and has come to his rescue in the nick of time. The LightFoot are in a circle and all have their spears drawn. One by one they are going to rush Fox and jab him with their weapon unless the CloudRunner can swoop down and flame them in time.

The CloudRunner doesn't have great aim and is going to rely on you to tell him when to attack. Watch the meter at the top of the screen and only press the Ⓐ Button when the red line is within the green zone. If the red line is stopped outside of the green zone or too late, the LightFoot will land their jab and Fox will suffer damage. However, if the Ⓐ

Button is pressed in time, the CloudRunner will swoop in and torch the LightFoot. Each time the CloudRunner fends off one of Fox's assailants, the green zone shrinks. By the time the final LightFoot is closing in on Fox, the green zone is incredibly small and it will require some quick reflexes to time the CloudRunner's flame properly.

Once the final LightFoot is sent searching for a fire extinguisher, the LightFoot Chief will agree to untie Fox (as long as the CloudRunner stops flaming his tribe members). The tribe decides they are better off ignoring Fox for the time being and head back to their huts.

LOOKING FOR KRAZOA SPIRITS PART 1

Since this area is typically off-limits to everyone, but tribal members, Fox should take the opportunity to look around. And there's no better place to start than on the ceremonial hilltop he finds himself on. This particular hill is ringed by a series of small brick crenulations, each with a wooden block inserted into it. That is, with the exception of three empty holes: a circle, a triangle, and a square. Perhaps Fox can win some favor

with the local tribe if he finds the missing blocks?

Descend the ladder and head southwest towards the wall. Look for the dried patch of dirt near the wall and have Tricky dig up the **Circle Block Carving**.

Swim across the pond to the north and follow the wall to the large briar patch. Give Tricky the "Flame" command here. In the alcove beyond the briars is another dirt patch. Put Tricky to work once again to uncover the **Square Block Carving**.

Head to the far northeastern corner and give Tricky his "Find Secret" command one more time. The prize this time is none other than the **Triangle Block Carving**. With all three Block Carvings in your possession, return to the top of the ceremonial hill and place them each in three openings bearing the same shape.

Descend the ladder once again and hop across the three tiny rock platforms to the island to the west. Flip over the blue speckled stone to reveal a Rocket Boost Pad and use it to leap to the top of the island. Cross the bridge to the neighboring hut and then descend the ladder so as to cross over to the Chief's hut in the northwest corner.

The Chief senses Fox's appreciation for Krazoa Spirits and offers to show him their underground chamber...so long as Fox completes the LightFoot Tests! It's just like Tricky says, "They're laughing at you Fox; you got to do it!"

THE TRACKING TEST

The first LightFoot Test is also the most difficult: activate the four Totem Poles faster than MuscleFoot's all-time best record of 2:30.

1 Climb the ladder back to the upper bridge and cross it back to the rock tower with the Totem Pole on it.

2 Run clockwise around the base of the ceremonial hill until the next Totem Pole comes into view. Swim across to the north bank and hop across the stepping-stones to reach it.

3 Use the Rocket Boost Pad in the alcove where the Square Block Carving was. The Totem Pole is smack in front of the landing area on the upper ledge.

4 Cross the pond to the southeast corner and climb up the moss-covered stone tower to the final Totem Pole standing atop it.

THE TEST OF STRENGTH

The Test of Strength pits Fox against MuscleFoot in a modified version of a tug of war. Press the (A) Button as fast as you can to have Fox push with all his might against the paddle so as to knock MuscleFoot into the pit. There are no special tricks involved in winning this Test, just very fast fingertips!

LOOKING FOR KRAZOA SPIRITS PART 2

After completing both LightFoot Tests, the Chief will declare Fox an honorary member of the LightFoot Tribe! And to welcome Fox into the tribe, the Chief opens the entrance to their underground chamber. Enter the chamber below the ceremonial hill and descend the ladder to the dirt-covered floor below.

The gate leading out of the room is currently barred shut, but the way to open it isn't far away. Load up on Energy Gems and climb to the top of the stack of yellow crates. Draw the Fire Blaster and step onto the black panel atop the uppermost crate. Whenever this panel is depressed the various segments of the totem pole in the center of the room will begin to rotate. Since they rotate independent of one another, and not all at the same time, the painting displayed on them is never straight. Shoot the Fire Blaster at the artwork on each section of the Totem to "paint" it white and to lock it in place. Shooting the same piece a second time will unlock it.

Continue locking pieces of the Totem into place until the entire Totem Pole is assembled. This will unlock the tunnel leading towards the Krazoa Shrine Entrance Warp.

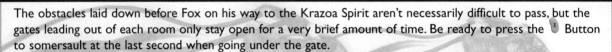

GOT ENERGY? TIP

Be sure and gather up some more Energy Gems before heading to the Krazoa Shrine; the very first thing Fox will have to do is use his Rocket Boost and there's no Magical Plants in the Shrine.

KRAZOA TEST

The obstacles laid down before Fox on his way to the Krazoa Spirit aren't necessarily difficult to pass, but the gates leading out of each room only stay open for a very brief amount of time. Be ready to press the Ⓧ Button to somersault at the last second when going under the gate.

1 Rocket Boost up to the first corridor. Once there, draw the Fire Blaster and take out the two gargoyles flying about. Step on the black panel to raise the gate across the room and then dodge the myriad of flames on your way to the next room.

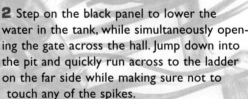

2 Step on the black panel to lower the water in the tank, while simultaneously opening the gate across the hall. Jump down into the pit and quickly run across to the ladder on the far side while making sure not to touch any of the spikes.

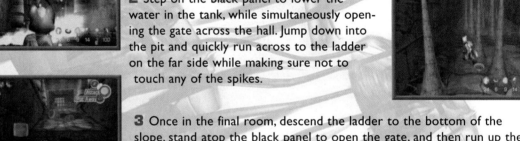

3 Once in the final room, descend the ladder to the bottom of the slope, stand atop the black panel to open the gate, and then run up the slope while dodging the barrels tumbling down at you.

The Test of Fear is very similar to the scene in which the CloudRunner was protecting Fox from the LightFoot and their spears. A meter will appear at the top of the screen with a green "safe zone" in it. This time,

instead of the red needle sliding back and forth across the meter, it will rather motionless… at first. As the fright-level heats up, the needle will begin to shake and move more readily. Use the ⚪ to keep the needle in the green area throughout the ordeal to complete the Test of Fear.

FOCUS   TIP

Like the Test of Strength, there aren't any cheats or tricks that can be used to outwit the Krazoa Spirit. Instead, you're just going to have to have a steady hand. One thing that does help, however, is refraining from looking at Fox or the action around him. Keep your eyes trained on the meter and make subtle adjustments to keep Fox from becoming afraid.

SEARCHING THE VILLAGE

Rumor has it that a Cheat Token Well can be found somewhere in LightFoot Village. Perhaps if Fox sticks around and helps his new tribe members with some minor chores, they'll let him know their secret.

Climb the ladder to the hut in the northeast corner of the pond and talk to the LightFoot inside. She'll explain that her babies are in the forest. Fox must bring them back home. Use the Rocket Boost Pad and turn to the east to find them. Now, all Fox has to do is chase them back towards the spot where he jumped up into the woods. Once all three are chased out of the forest, return to the LightFoot for a reward. To show her gratitude, she'll open a hut containing multiple SharpClaw Crates.

Visit the hut nearest the Chief's to find out where her kids may be hiding. "My babies like to climb trees", she'll say. Finding this set of babies requires Fox to think outside of the box, err, walls. Exit the village and defeat the SharpClaw milling around in the outer area. Strike the trees near the entrance to Cape Claw with the Staff to shake the babies off the branches above. The babies are in the three trees near the large rocks with the Scarabs underneath.

Although the first two rewards might not have be worth the effort, the third LightFoot mommy is sure to give Fox some-

thing he wants—like access to the Cheat Token Well! Cross the bridge to the hut nearby. This mother will explain that her kids are "so naughty" and they like to play underground. Enter the doorway at the base of the ceremonial hill to find her three children running around the upper walkway inside the hill. Chase them back around towards the exit to send them on their way back to their mom. This LightFoot mother will show her appreciation by placing several SharpClaw Crates on top of the ceremonial hill.

NOTE   REENTERING LIGHTFOOT VILLAGE

The gate may have slammed behind you but Fox can still get back into the Village. Notice the three trees with the tribal rings on them? These trees act as a doorbell of sorts and need to be struck in a certain order. Use the Staff to "ring" the tree nearest the gate, followed by the one furthest from the gate, and finally the middle tree.

Hurry back to the third LightFoot family's hut to be given your reward; the Rocket Boost Pad near the gate is now activated! Cross back to the gate and use the Rocket Boost to leap onto the wall along the south side of the village. Now Fox can travel through the northeastern section of the forest to find the **Cheat Token Well**, a **Fuel Cell**, and a **BafomDad**!

Return to ThornTail Hollow and have the WarpStone send you back to Krazoa Palace.

KRAZOA PALACE

Now that Fox has been here once before, and has proven himself worthy of entering the Palace, the WarpStone sends him directly to the room adjacent the one with the enormous fans. Ride the pedestal up to the upper hallway and approach the large fans.

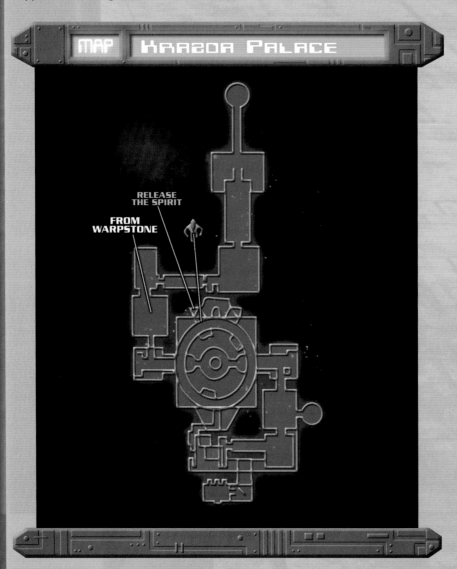

MAP KRAZOA PALACE

RELEASE THE SPIRIT

FROM WARPSTONE

Float on the updrafts up to the second highest walkway and circle around to the north to find a SharpClaw Pad. Put on the Disguise and step onto the Pad to open the door. Step onto the glowing pedestal to release the third Krazoa Spirit.

SPELLSTONE #3

FINDING THE THIRD SPELLSTONE

Everything may look on the "up and up" back at the Hollow, but it's far from the truth. The lady ThornTail who lives in the cave near the WarpStone isn't just being paranoid anymore. She's really in trouble! Rush over to her rescue.

THORNTAIL HOLLOW

SAVE THE THORNTAIL EGGS

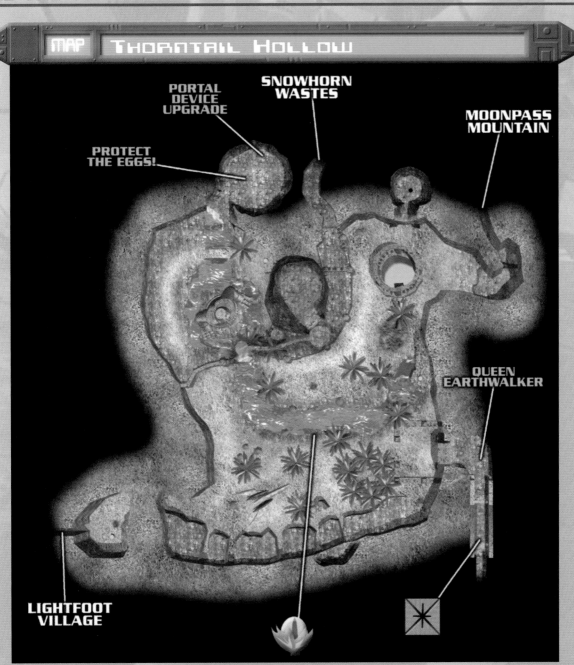

MAP THORNTAIL HOLLOW

PORTAL DEVICE UPGRADE

SNOWHORN WASTES

MOONPASS MOUNTAIN

PROTECT THE EGGS!

QUEEN EARTHWALKER

LIGHTFOOT VILLAGE

115

Enter the cave to start the timer. Fox must protect the five ThornTail eggs in the center of the cave from being stolen for 1:40. The egg-nappers will emerge from each of the four tunnels in the sides of the cave and will slither down the chutes towards the nest. Fox must strike them down with the Staff (one swing is all it takes) in order to protect the eggs. If so much as one egg gets stolen, Fox will have to start over.

Although the creatures come just one at a time, more and more make a run for the eggs as time goes by. Once there are less than thirty seconds left on the clock, it becomes an absolute Staff-swinging frenzy as nearly a dozen thieves will be going for the eggs at the same time. The key to successfully defending the eggs is to stay near the nest and rely on the length of the Staff to belt any thief that comes near. Also, by staying close to the nest, and resisting being pulled away, Fox will be able to smash multiple enemies with a single swipe. Additionally, using the Ground Quake will clear the screen of enemies. Use whichever you prefer.

As a reward for saving her eggs, the ThornTail reveals an entrance to an underground power-up location that was hidden inside her cave. Drop down the hole to obtain the **Portal Device** upgrade. This upgrade will allow Fox to use the Staff to open the large beige doors that he has no doubt seen throughout Dinosaur Planet.

Exit the cave and head back to the Queen EarthWalker's temple. The Queen informs Fox and Tricky that Tricky's dad is locked within the walls of the Walled City, and to make matters worse, he is the GateKeeper to the Walled City! He was smart enough to hide his GateKeeper powers behind the seal in the temple. Approach the seal and use the Portal Device to open it. Now Fox can make the journey to the Walled City!

116

NOTE **Don't Forget the Map**

Head back to the ThornTail Store before heading off to space, you'll want the **Walled City Map** when you get there!

SPACE TRAVEL

DESTINATION: WALLED CITY

Fuel Cells Needed: 12

Gold Rings: 7 of 10

Time: 1:00

The Walled City is composed of large temples and monuments, many of which have fallen off into space during the land's removal from Dinosaur Planet. This flight is a lot more dangerous than previous ones, so be sure to not miss any of the Silver Rings and try to collect each of the Bomb Upgrades—they'll come in handy when going through the mine fields.

1 Keep to the center as the Arwing reaches the first crumbled temple.

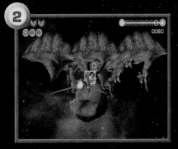

2 Aim for the central arch on the underside of the large rock island. Fly over the asteroid to be in the right position for it.

3 Just past the rock island is an upside-down temple with a narrow corridor running through its center. Shoot out the "X" in the Gold Ring in this corridor.

4 Navigate the corridor and fly upwards towards the arch in the rocks after exiting the temple.

5 Bear to the right while approaching the next large set of ruins. Fly through the circle of stone on the right to get the fifth Gold Ring.

6 Immediately after #5, break hard to the left to get the next Gold Ring in a similar circle of stone.

7 Fly through the doors straight ahead and head to the right of the columns inside the ruins to find the next Gold Ring.

JET SET   TIP

Be sure to use the Arwing's speed burst (🖱 Button) when flying through the metal doors, as there's not much time to make it through unscathed.

WALLED CITY

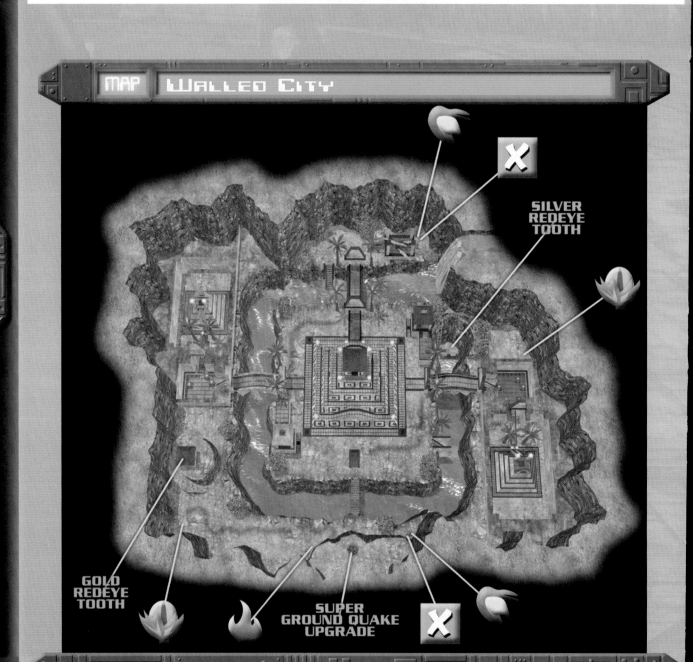

MAP   WALLED CITY

SILVER REDEYE TOOTH

GOLD REDEYE TOOTH

SUPER GROUND QUAKE UPGRADE

The Walled City has become the private stomping ground of the RedEye Tribe—the most vicious dinosaur tribe on the entire planet. Fox doesn't need to worry about them just yet, though. He was smart enough to land the Arwing on a narrow stretch of land across the river from the RedEyes.

Step down off the landing platform and have Tricky dig up the **BafomDad** to the east of the Arwing. Head back around to the west and approach the EarthWalker stationed by the tree. This particular EarthWalker isn't of much importance to Fox, but the orange panel in the tree is! Use the Fire Blaster to shoot the panel to light one of the flames on the platform by the Arwing.

Cross the moat via the bridge near the EarthWalker and carefully skirt past the RedEyes towards the small monument in the southwest

corner. Locate the blue tablet depicting the moon and perform a Ground Quake atop within the ring of blue light on the ground. This will raise the fire well on the monument above. Fox has 2:00 to race through the temple's "moon" corridor to this monument and have Tricky light the well with his "Flame" command.

Dash back around to the northern side of the temple and follow the walkway up and to the right. Continue past the sliding blocks and up to the next level. Run past the entrance to the red "sun" corridor and over the next walkway ramp to reach the "moon" passage. Somersault through the blue flames and up to the fire well where Tricky can light the flame.

This will make the moon depiction in the platform south of the tunnel begin to glow.

Now it's time to do the same for the red "sun" monument. Return to the northeastern corner of the temple where the red monument is and perform another Ground Quake within the ring of light. Once again, Fox has 2:00 to navigate the temple's corridors to reach the red monument. Once there, have Tricky light the flame to light the sun panel in the platform south of the temple. This will reveal a hidden passage leading below the temple.

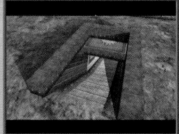

Inside the underground passage is King EarthWalker. He knows all about Fox's mission and provides council as to where Fox may find the SpellStone. He tells Fox that he will need to find two Sacred Teeth to enter the "lair of the RedEye King". That's not all; there is a magic cave nearby—possibly over the bridge to the south—that has the solution for battling the RedEye Tribe members!

119

ENTERING THE REDEYE KING'S LAIR

Cross the moat via the recently repaired wooden bridge to the south and approach the EarthWalker on the left. Shoot the orange panel in the tree near him to light another flame by the Arwing. This EarthWalker provides Fox with sound advice, "look for other EarthWalkers". Wherever there is an EarthWalker, Fox will find another orange panel to shoot. There are a total of four of them to find. Two down, two to go!

Have Tricky dig up another **BafomDad** near the tree behind the EarthWalker and then head back to the west to find the briars. Have Tricky burn the briars off the rocks so Fox can climb up to the ledge above. There he will find a Bomb Spore Planting Patch that he can utilize to blow an opening into the underground power-up location below. Drop into the hole to gain the **Super Ground Quake** upgrade. This enhancement to the Staff will allow Fox to wield such deadly force that even the RedEyes will be brought to their knees.

Exit the cave and continue west along this stretch of land towards another Bomb Spore Planting Patch. Detonating a Bomb Spore here will reveal a cave containing another **BafomDad** as well as some Scarabs.

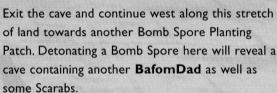

Continue following the outlying piece of land clockwise around the Walled City until coming to the third EarthWalker. He, too, is standing next to a tree with an orange panel in it as well.

There's only one more orange panel to find and it's in the northeastern corner of the map. Head around the red monument to find the fourth EarthWalker and shoot the panel in the tree to reveal the "secret of the river".

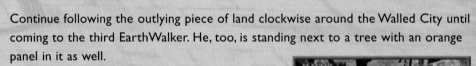

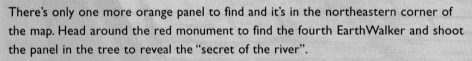

THE SECRET OF THE RIVER

Once all four of the orange panels have been hit with the Fire Blaster, return to the Arwing and jump into the water near the waterfall. Swim through the sparkling ring of light by the water surface to start a timer. The timer will start with just 0:17 on it, so Fox had better get swimming fast!

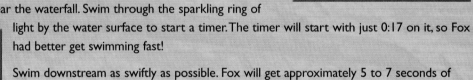

Swim downstream as swiftly as possible. Fox will get approximately 5 to 7 seconds of bonus time for each sparkling ring he swims through. He must swim through nine of these rings in order to have enough time to open the lockbox in the room at the end of the river.

Inside the lockbox, Fox will discover the **Silver RedEye Tooth**. Return to the underground room where the King is waiting and place the tooth in the right-hand RedEye statue.

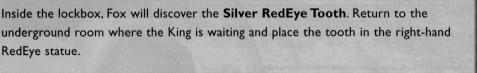

THE REDEYE LIFE FORCE

Load up on Energy Gems and assign the Fire Blast to the  Button—it's time to go dino hunting! There are a total of four RedEyes needing to be put down, one on each side of the temple. Use the Super Ground Quake to knock them on their sides and then quickly grab the Fire Blaster and finish them off. Depending on how many rounds from the

Fire Blaster hit their mark, this process may have to be repeated twice per RedEye. There are two Fuel Barrel generators next to the Ground Quake pods that can also be of use.

Once all four RedEye are defeated, the Life-Force Door atop the hill in the southwest corner will open. Climb the spiraling path to the top of the hill and open the lockbox to find the **Gold RedEye Tooth**. Return to the King's underground area and place the tooth in the RedEye statue on the left. With both of the sacred teeth in place, Fox is ready to descend into the RedEye Lair.

THE REDEYE KING'S LAIR

BOSS BATTLE: REDEYE KING

The RedEye King's Lair consists of a square-shaped, narrow corridor with extremely tall walls. Anything else wouldn't accommodate the oversized dinosaur. In each of the inside corners is a small alcove that can be accessed by shooting the orange panel above. Inside, Fox will find a **Fuel Barrel Generator** as well as a DumbleDang Pod. Each stretch of the corridor also has a small alcove where Magical Plants grow.

Helpful items aren't the only things to be found in the Lair, however. Each section of hallway contains a pair of panels in the floor that, when depressed, emits a high-voltage current that arcs across the hall, electrifying anything caught in its path. This system was installed as a means of keeping the RedEye under control, as it is the only thing powerful enough in all of Dinosaur Planet to restrain the RedEye King.

NOTE | ALTERNATING HALLWAYS

The same electric shock system cannot be used twice in a row after a failed attempt. Once used, a hallway's system will stay powered-down until Fox steps on the electric panels in either of the adjacent hallways.

As big and fearsome as the RedEye King is, this battle is surprisingly very straightforward; then again, RedEyes are certainly the least intelligent of all the tribes! The RedEye King is monstrous. Additionally, whenever rounding a turn and entering a new hall, the beast will come to a halt and let out a deafening roar. Surprise attacks are definitely not his forte!

NOTE   MY, WHAT BIG FEET YOU HAVE!

Although the RedEye King is unlikely to catch Fox off guard, there will come a time when Fox undoubtedly gets stepped on or hit with the RedEye King's head or tail. These are the RedEye King's only ways of inflicting damage and Fox will lose two blocks of energy every time he comes into contact with the beast. Be sure and smash those casks for the DumbleDang Pods, as two blocks of energy here and there can add up quickly!

To destroy the beast Fox must grab a Fuel Barrel and wait near the electric panel at the opposite end of the hall from where the RedEye King appears. Wait until he is just about to finish his roar and then step forward onto the electric panel to begin charging the system. If timed properly, the electric current will shoot across the room just as the RedEye King is walking by. The dose of high-voltage will send him to the floor, at which time Fox must then throw the Fuel Barrel at his head.

Once a successful hit is made on the RedEye King, that hallway's electric panels will fade away and Fox will have to head to one of the other sides of the corridor. Repeat this very same attack pattern until the RedEye King has been hit four times. Once the Boss is down for the count, Fox will be able to pry the second **Fire SpellStone** from the top of the beast's head.

Tricky's father, King EarthWalker, walks the two adventurers back to the Arwing and wishes them luck in returning the SpellStone to Volcano Force Point Temple. Unfortunately for Tricky, however, King EarthWalker is sworn to wait at the Walled City until the planet is pieced back together. Thanks to Fox and Tricky, that shouldn't be too long from now!

NOTE   FLYING HOME

The flight back to Dinosaur Planet is always the same: no Fuel Cells are consumed and the Arwing only needs to be flown through 1 Gold Ring to open the Force Field. See the first *ThornTail Hollow* chapter for tips on Gold Ring location.

Delivering the Third SpellStone

Volcano Force Point Temple Part 1

MAP   Volcano Force Point Temple

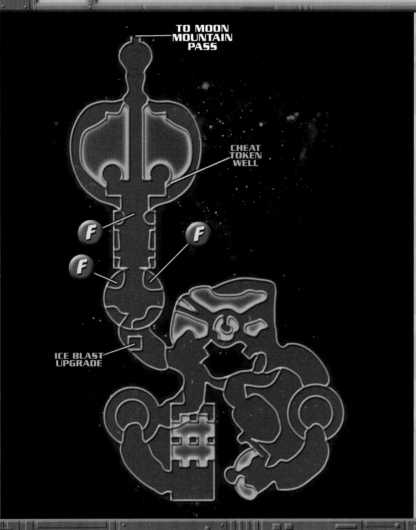

TO MOON
MOUNTAIN
PASS

CHEAT
TOKEN
WELL

F

F

F

ICE BLAST
UPGRADE

Make the trek from ThornTail Hollow back through Moon Mountain Pass and into the tomb leading towards Volcano Force Point Temple. Approach the left-hand ledge outside the main entrance to the Temple and drop down towards the lava. Plant a MoonSeed in the patch near the wall and climb up to the Cheat Token Well above. Along the way, put the SharpClaw Disguise to good use and open up the third and final cage in the central lava room. There, Fox will find a **BafomDad** and two **Fuel Cells**.

Since Fox has already passed through here once, he doesn't need to light the various orbs at the main gate. Instead, he just needs to show the SpellStone and he'll be permitted inside. The same is true for the Life-Force Door; it's no longer here. Nevertheless, as Fox continues onward through the Temple and finds the route open to him, it's worthwhile to look around. For example, there are two **Fuel Cells** to be had by climbing the ladder in the circular room and following the balcony around to the other side.

Ride the lift down the lower level and head to the central room where the pair of SpellStone slots are. Use the Ice Blast to extinguish the flame leaping up through the grate and place the SpellStone in the slot opposite where you enter the room. Although the door that unlocks seems unreachable at first, Fox can jump down onto the blocks floating in the lava and hop across to the rock wall leading up to the doorway.

BURNING FEET   TIP

Fox can actually run through the lava without losing too much health thanks to the sixth Energy Badge he was awarded at Walled City!

Dodge the flames in the next passage and ride the lift upwards. Since this is an area Fox has yet to explore, there's a new puzzle waiting for him at the top.

A RAINBOW OF COLOR

The door leading to the final warp pad is bolted shut and will not open until Fox extinguishes the flames atop the upper ledge. Which, if you've tried, is no easy task since the flames re-ignite moments later. Or do they?

Proceed towards the large door at the end of the tunnel, being careful to note the color of the torches on the walls. The colors of the flames are as follows: blue, green, red, yellow. This is the order in which the flames on the balcony must be doused. Any deviation will result in all the flames reigniting. Once the four flames have all been extinguished, the door will unlock and Fox can proceed to the next room.

VOLCANO FORCE POINT TEMPLE PART 2

Defeat the two SharpClaw in the next room and have Tricky "Stay" on the panel that rises up out of the floor. Climb the ladder with Fox and extinguish the flame with the Ice Blast. Flip the switch on the wall and return to Tricky on the ground below.

The final room before the warp pad contains three orbs that must be hit while Fox is floating back and forth across the room on a large block. Have Tricky hold the panel down while Fox extinguishes the flame on the block and then jump onto it. Grab the Fire Blaster and train your eyes on the blue, green, and blue orbs near the ceiling. Shoot the Fire Blaster through the flame in the center of the lava pool and into each of the orbs. Concentrate on just one orb at a time and wait for the block to float into the proper position.

Use the warp pad in the next room to enter the upper part of the temple where the SpellStones are placed. There's only one left now, you're almost done!

SPELLSTONE #4

FINDING THE FOURTH SPELLSTONE

Fox gets back to ThornTail Hollow just in time to help fend off a horde of bat-like creatures that are harassing the peaceful ThornTails. Grab the Fire Blaster and head to their rescue!

THORNTAIL HOLLOW

SAVE THE THORNTAILS

MAP ThornTail Hollow

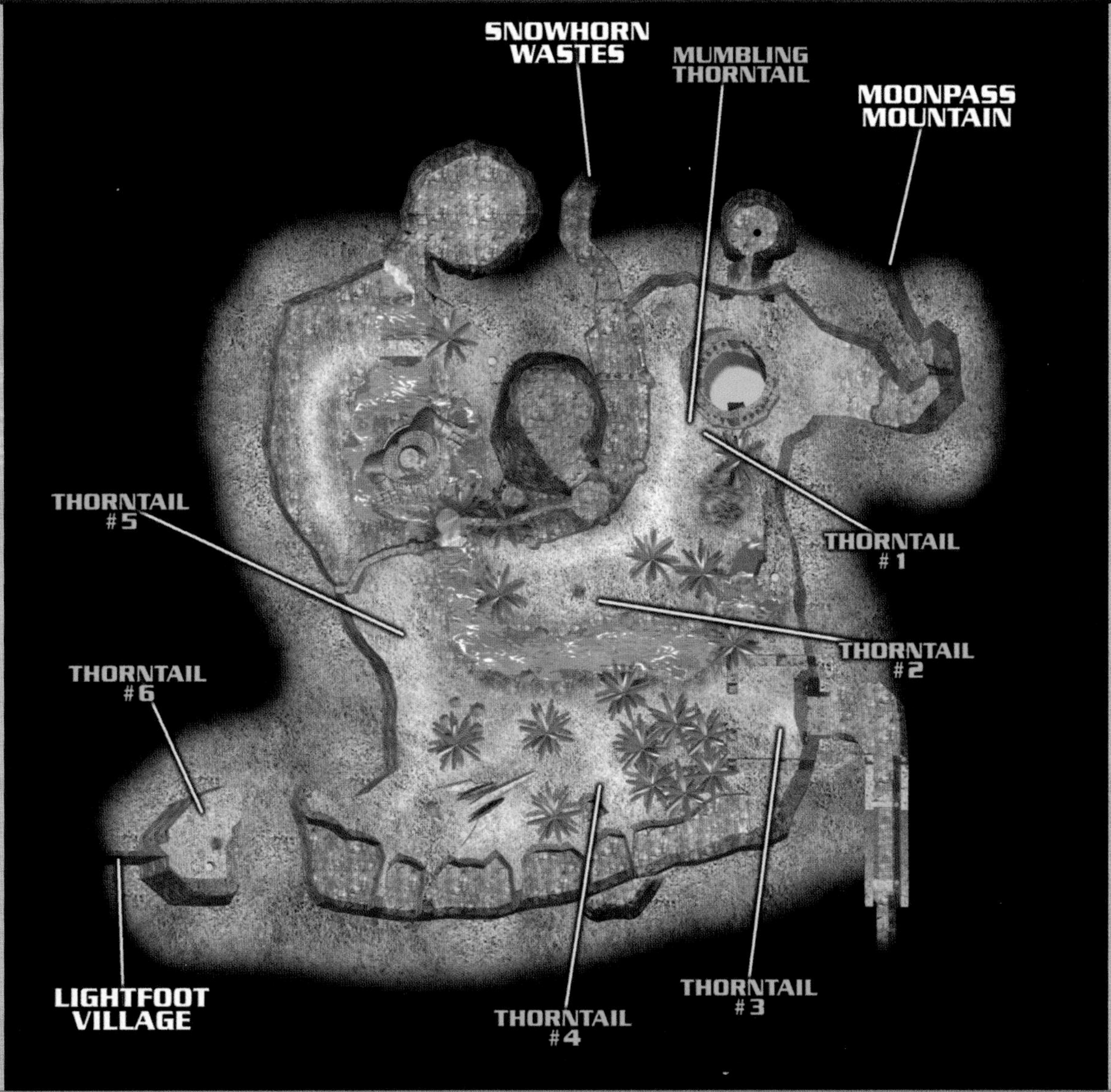

SNOWHORN
WASTES

MUMBLING
THORNTAIL

MOONPASS
MOUNTAIN

THORNTAIL
#5

THORNTAIL
#1

THORNTAIL
#6

THORNTAIL
#2

LIGHTFOOT
VILLAGE

THORNTAIL
#4

THORNTAIL
#3

125

Fox hasn't got much time in order to save the ThornTails from the infestation of bats! There are a total of six ThornTails under duress. Hurry to each of them and use the Fire Blaster to destroy the three bats that hover above each of them.

1 The first ThornTail is in front of the ancient well.

2 Head towards the ThornTail Store. The next ThornTail is by the river in front of the shop's entrance.

3 Cross the river and head east to the Queen's temple. One of her ThornTail followers is being harassed in the courtyard.

4 The fourth ThornTail is near the nose of the Arwing.

5 Start up the path towards the WarpStone. There's another endangered ThornTail just south of the wall.

Make a quick dash back down the hill and onto the path leading towards LightFoot Village. The final ThornTail is right outside the Hollow's main area.

6 Once all six ThornTail are safe and the 18 bats have been eliminated, Fox will be given a reward: the **Large Scarab Bag**! This is the biggest Scarab Bag in all of Dinosaur Planet and it can store up to 200 Scarabs! Put it to use right away by digging up Scarabs in the circle of rocks or by wagering the ones Fox already has in the Scarab Game. Either way, be sure to buy the **SnowHorn Artifact** from the ShopKeeper. He's trying to sell it for 130 Scarabs, but Fox may be able to buy it for just 120 Scarabs.

There's somebody back in the SnowHorn Wastes who has really been looking for his "golden root". Hurry back through the Sewers to see if the SnowHorn Artifact belongs to him.

126

SnowHorn Wastes

The Call of the SnowHorn

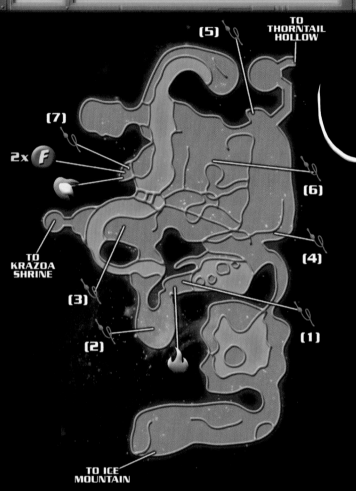

MAP SnowHorn Wastes

The SnowHorn by the lake is ecstatic to see his golden root returned to him after all these years and, as a reward, he gives Fox the chance to prove himself. A series of seven Horn Pads will appear one after the other as Fox sounds the Dinosaur Horn on each of them. A special gift will await Fox at the end of the challenge.

Exploring Ahead TIP

Since this is a timed challenge, Fox would be well served to scout ahead and remove some of the time-consuming barriers. For starters, have Tricky "Flame" the wall of ice behind the SnowHorn. Just further down the trail there is a large dead tree with a gaping hole in its side. Shoot this tree with the Fire Blaster to make it fall across the river, thus giving Fox a bridge. There is another tree further along the route, but Fox should have plenty of time accumulated by then. Assign the Dinosaur Horn to the 🅨 Button.

1 Blow the Horn atop the Horn Pad near the SnowHorn to begin the challenge, Fox will have 0:50 to reach the next Horn pad.

2 Head through the archway behind the SnowHorn (Tricky must "Flame" the ice first) and approach the campfire down the hill to locate the next Horn pad.

3 Continue following this path past the stream (shoot the hole in the tree with the Fire Blaster to knock the tree down) to the Horn Pad near the large river.

4 Turn from the river and head south past the fence and the SharpClaw and off the small cliff and down towards the SnowHorns.

5 Head due east past the entrance to the sewers, to the tiny alcove beyond it.

6 Sprint back towards the prison area where Garunda Te was being held. The next Horn Pad is right above his former cell.

7 Loop around the fence by the river near Garunda Te and approach the tall tree to the west. Fell the tree with the Fire Blaster and climb the rocks across the river to the Horn Pad.

Once Fox blows the Dinosaur Horn on the final pad, a gate to a previously unseen Krazoa Shrine Entrance Warp is revealed. Grab the two **Fuel Cells** next to the Warp Pad and smash the SharpClaw Crate for an extra **BafomDad**.

Return back to where Horn Pad #3 was located and swim across the icy river to the silver SnowHorn on the far side. Enter small room and warp to the next Krazoa Shrine.

128

KRAZOA TEST

This Krazoa Shrine has slightly more complex obstacles leading to the Krazoa Spirit. But what's even more challenging is the Test of Strength. This is the most difficult Krazoa Test of all.

1 Use the Fire Blaster to take out the bats before grabbing the **Fuel Barrel**. With the room clear, carry the explosive across the narrow path and detonate it against the far wall.

2 Carry a second Fuel Barrel into the next room and place it down on the Fuel Barrel Pad. Flip the switch to shut off the first flame jet and wait for the magnetic lift to start to turn to the right. As soon as it does, flip the switch again to turn back on the first flame.

3 Guide the Fuel Barrel through the corner updraft and quickly place it down on the Fuel Barrel Pad before the SharpClaw gets to it. Destroy the SharpClaw and then grab the Fuel Barrel and throw it at the far wall.

The Test of Strength is very similar to the LightFoot Test in which Fox had to push against MuscleFoot. Here, Fox must go up against a SharpClaw. Press the Ⓐ Button as fast as you can to push the large slab one-half rotation while trying to overcome the SharpClaw's efforts to push against you. Fox has 1:06 to defeat the SharpClaw in this Test else he'll have to navigate the Shrine's obstacles once again. As was the case with defeating MuscleFoot, there are no tricks to beating the SharpClaw other than pushing the Ⓐ Button really, really fast.

With the fourth Krazoa Spirit safe inside Fox's fur, it's time to head to the Krazoa Palace. Return through the Sewers and have the WarpStone transport you to the Palace.

129

KRAZOA PALACE

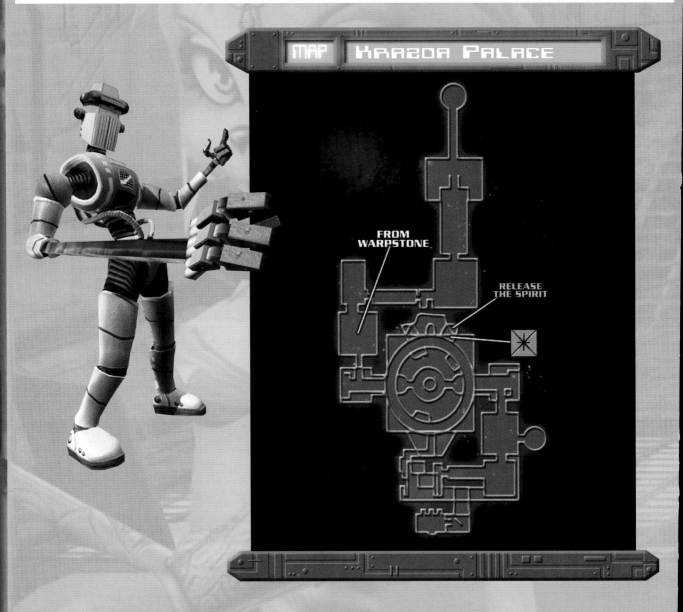

MAP **KRAZOA PALACE**

FROM
WARPSTONE

RELEASE
THE SPIRIT

130

Ride the lift up to the upper hallway and head left to ride the winds of the mega-fans once again. Fox only needs to ride to the updrafts to the floor just above the one he enters on. Head to the northeast corner and use the Portal Device to open up the alcove where the Krazoa Spirit must be released.

THORNTAIL HOLLOW

A TROUBLED THORNTAIL

There's a ThornTail in the Hollow that is quite distraught. Seek out the ThornTail that always mumbled when Fox approached; he's finally ready to tell his story. He's the one located between the ancient well and the ThornTail Store.

As it turns out, long before Fox ever touched down on Dinosaur Planet, this troubled ThornTail led an attack against General Scales—and was massacred. General Scales launched a surprise counter-attack and fled with the SpellStone and many of the other ThornTails. This particular ThornTail was left alive because he is the GateKeeper. And with a flourish, he opens the gate to Dragon Rock for Fox.

NOTE — Don't Forget the Map

Head back to the ThornTail Store and purchase the **Dragon Rock Map** before blasting off into space.

SPACE TRAVEL

DESTINATION: DRAGON ROCK

The flight to Dragon Rock is the most difficult journey Fox must take during his quest to rebuild Dinosaur Planet. Not only must he fly through all 10 Gold Rings, but some of the large asteroids and islands have multiple paths through them. Lastly, the opposition has littered this route with more mines than Fox has ever seen in all his days in the Lylat System.

- ● **Fuel Cells Needed: 15**
- ● **Gold Rings: 10 of 10**
- ● **Time: 1:00**

1 Keep to the right-hand side of the island as the first Gold Ring is off to the side, just past it.

SPACE TRAVEL

2 Dive into the opening of the lengthy pipe and hold the Arwing down low to grab the next Gold Ring.

3 Turbo into the asteroid ahead but quickly put on the reverse thrusters to better locate the next Gold Ring.

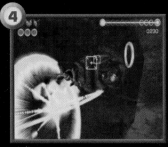

4 The next Gold Ring is in the same cave as #3. Keep flying slowly and turbo through its center.

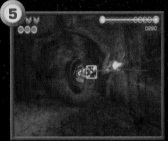

5 Take either route when the cave forks up ahead. The next Gold Ring is located where the paths reunite.

6 Exit the cave and fly up and to the left to grab the next Gold Ring.

7 Immediately dive down through the lower arch in the center of the island and hit the brakes. The next Gold Ring is just ahead.

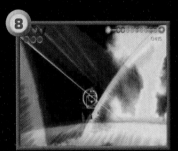

8 Enter the pipe up ahead and blast through the other spacecraft to reach the eighth Gold Ring in one piece.

9 The ninth Gold Ring is deceptively hard to fly through as it is positioned relatively alone in space and moves around in spurts.

10 Enter the large tunnel up ahead and stick to the center; you're home free!

DRAGON ROCK

GIDDY UP EARTHWALKER!

SHIELD GENERATOR

HIGHTOP

SHIELD GENERATOR

TO DRAKOR

SHIELD GENERATOR

SHIELD GENERATOR

SHIELD GENERATOR

EARTHWALKER

CLOUDRUNNER

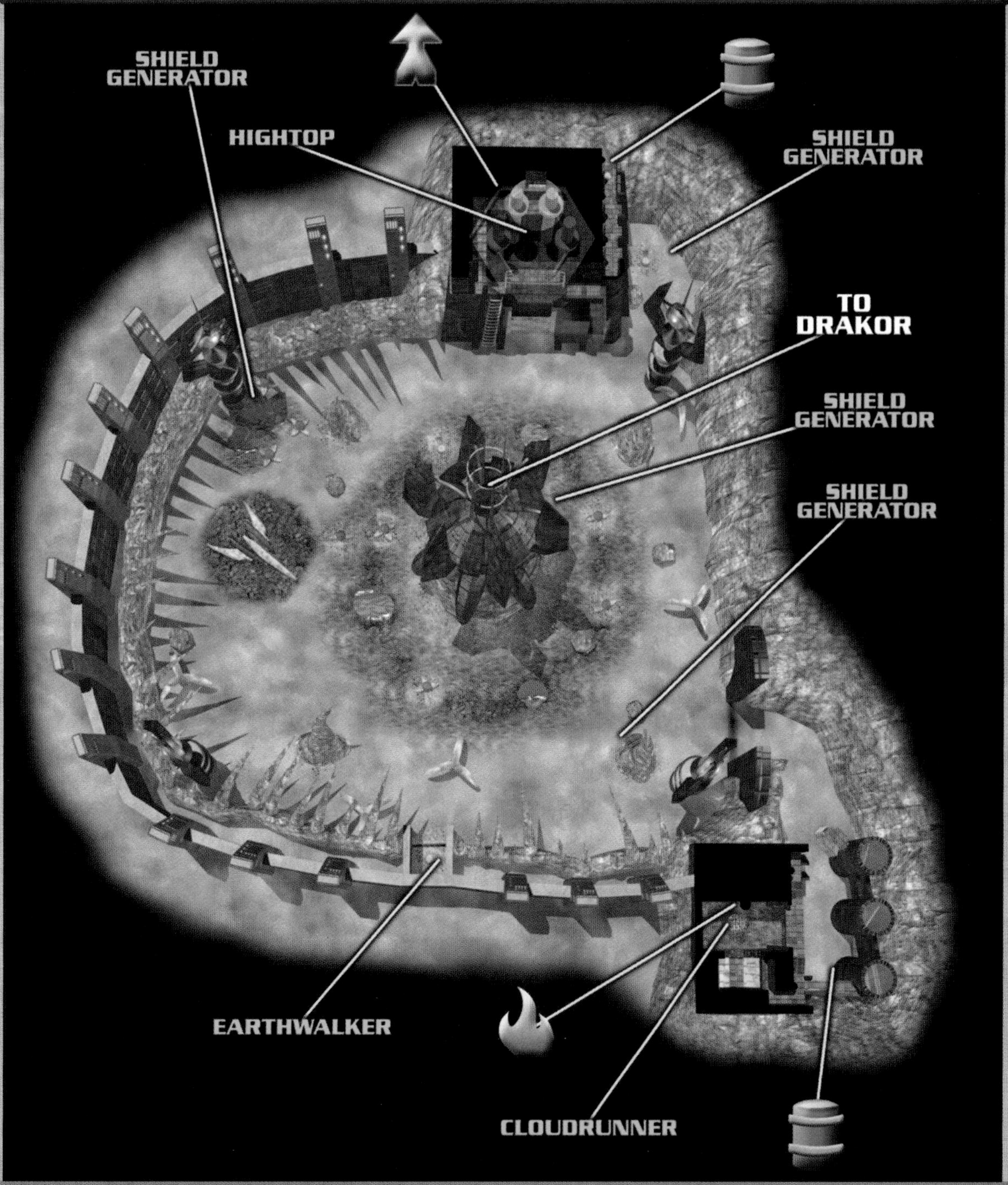

It is clear from the moment Fox steps out of the Arwing that Dragon Rock is not friendly territory. And despite the danger lurking nearly everywhere, both the plants and the hovering security guns are indestructible at this time.

Circle around to the north part of the Rock by ducking behind the various rock spires whenever a security gun floats near. Make a break for the ladder and climb it to the ledge above. Once on top, Fox will find another ladder to the right. The uppermost ledge contains a pair of floor panels that, when depressed, turn off the flames next to them. Keep moving along the ledge in a counter-clockwise direction to the far end where the **Fuel Barrel** is located.

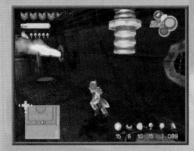

Carry the Fuel Barrel back to the Fuel Barrel Pad and set it down. Flip the switch to call for the magnetic lift and quickly climb the short ladder to the upper platform. Fox must hold down the panels to turn the flames off as the Fuel Barrel is transported to the western edge of this tower.

FANCY CAMERAWORK TIP

Be sure to manipulate the camera so it's facing north instead of behind Fox. This will allow you to see exactly when it's safe to step off the panels.

Use the Fuel Barrel to destroy the wooden barricade and head inside. Follow the corridor to a switch that controls a large gate outside. Flip the switch to release a captured EarthWalker and head exit the tower. Cross the open field outside to where the EarthWalker is.

In order to make it safe for the capture HighTop to exit this place, the shields on the hovering security guns need to be destroyed. Mount the EarthWalker and take off in search of the power supplies controlling the shields. Perform a lap around the complex looking for cracks in the rocks with a green, glowing panel of light. Press the Ⓐ Button to have the EarthWalker smash the panel, thus turning off the shield to the security guns.

There are four power supplies that need to be destroyed (see map for specific locations). Once one has been smashed, locate the nearest platform where Fox can dismount from the EarthWalker and use the Fire Blaster to destroy the defenseless gun.

TAKIN' IT ONE DRONE AT A TIME   TIP

Although Fox is safe from danger while riding the EarthWalker, the same cannot be said for his prehistoric companion. Since the EarthWalker has a finite source of energy, care must be taken to keep him from harm. One way to do this is by eliminating each hovering gun as soon as its energy shield has been destroyed. This will reduce the chance of the EarthWalker being caught in crossfire.

UNLACING THE HIGHTOP

Once all four security drones have been destroyed, return the EarthWalker to where Fox originally found him and head back to the north tower. Enter through the ground level door on the right-hand side of the tower and follow the hall to the bound HighTop.

The poor HighTop, who probably never hurt a fly, has four super-thick energy cables around its neck; the poor guy can't even move! Shoot each of the four orange panels on the nearby poles to turn off the ropes one by one. This has to be done pretty swiftly, however, as the ropes will turn themselves back on after just 7 seconds. And each time a rope reappears around the HighTop's neck, the enormous beast slams the ground in anger, sending out a large distracting shockwave that undoubtedly throws off Fox's aim.

Smash the crate left of the HighTop's tail to reveal a Rocket Boost Pad. Use the Rocket Boost to reach the upper walkway and head around to the front of the imprisoned creature. From that vantage point, Fox will have an easier time shooting all four orange panels in time, but will also be less affected by the HighTop's shaking.

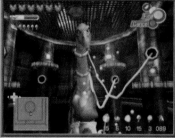

The HighTop doesn't waste anytime in making his escape plans: Fox must ride across the plain on his back while using the Fire Blaster to protect him from incoming missiles. The missiles will launch from the top of the central tower and Fox must shoot them before they slam into the HighTop. Although Fox cannot take damage during this scene (nor will his Staff run out of energy), the HighTop can.

135

Thanks to the HighTop's pedestrian pace, Fox is forced to protect him for nearly three minutes! The missiles will originally come in bursts of three, but will quickly grow to a grand finale in which nearly 30 missiles appear at once! Resist the tendency to fire off a barrage of random blasts, as it will not help the HighTop remain safe. Instead, do your best to aim for each missile as it closes in and blast it out of the sky with a single, well-aimed shot. Of course, once there's more than a dozen or so taking flight at once, this becomes more difficult. At this point, focus on the area immediately near the HighTop and sweep side to side while firing the Fire Blaster as fast as you can. This will effectively provide a protective barrier for the dinosaur and will greatly reduce the number of missiles that hit him, if any.

Once across the plain, the HighTop will press a switch high on a wall that will give Fox and Tricky access to another area of Dragon Rock.

CAGED BIRDS CAN'T FLY

The area on the other side of the gate contains a very unhappy CloudRunner pent up in a suspended cage. It's up to Fox to bust him out! And there's going to be a lot of "busting" involved!

Have Tricky "Stay" on the panel near the **Fuel Barrel** to the south. This will allow Fox to shoot each of the three orange panels below the flames to turn them off as the magnetic lift transports the Fuel Barrel across the yard. Stand in front of the middle flame and take aim with the Fire Blaster. Each flame will only stay extinguished for 6 seconds before reigniting so don't shoot the panels too prematurely.

Climb the ladder up to the Fuel Barrel and toss it through the updraft to the ledge on the other side, while being careful not to let it hit the flames! There is a total of three windy towers that Fox must float the Fuel Barrel across. Study the pattern of the flames in each of them and only throw the Fuel Barrel after the flames disappear. Use the explosives to blow up the wooden barricade blocking the hall on the left.

NOTE   GET THE BAFOMDAD

Before heading through the opening towards the CloudRunner, follow the ledge to the right towards the SharpClaw Crate. There's a **BafomDad** inside of it; this is something sure to prove useful as Fox gets closer to completing his mission.

138

Drop down into the small area facing the birdcage and flip the switch. This will cause the cage to slide back and forth along an overhead track. Use the Staff to flip the switch a second time once the cage's rope is directly in front of the black hole on the opposite wall. Once the cage is in the proper position, jump down and have Tricky "Flame" the red grate. This will cause a flame to shoot out the hole and burn through the rope, thus freeing the CloudRunner.

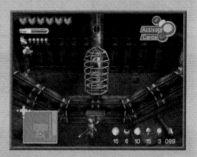

The caged CloudRunner turns out to be a friend of Krystal and knows all about the SpellStones. He agrees to help Fox get inside the Great Tower in the center of Dragon Rock, but to do so requires destroying the four spires that guard the perimeter first. Hop aboard the CloudRunner's back and prepare for one of the loftiest challenges in the game.

The CloudRunner is going to fly around the plain in a clockwise circle while Fox uses the Fire Blaster to protect them from the incoming missiles. Once the CloudRunner swoops in close to the spire, Fox must then train his site on the red orb on top. Surprisingly, as difficult as shooting down all of the 30+ missiles that launch from each spire is, destroying the red orb is equally as tough.

As was the case with the HighTop earlier, the CloudRunner has a finite energy meter and can eventually be shot down if Fox lets too many missiles through to their target. Unlike before, however, Fox's best chance at protecting the CloudRunner is by rapidly firing the Fire Blaster in a chaotic frenzy. This is the best way to counter the large numbers of missiles being launched simultaneously, as well as the unpredictable flight path of the CloudRunner.

NOTE — MISSILES, MISSILES, EVERYWHERE!

The CloudRunner will continue to swoop in close to each spire even if it has already been destroyed. While this may sound harmless enough, it's not. Each spire's missiles will continue to be launched until all four spires are destroyed. Fox and the CloudRunner get no reprieve from the onslaught!

RAPID FIRE TIP

The only way to succeed in this challenge is to train your site on the red orb as soon as possible (possibly between batches of missiles), and attack it with all the intensity needed to win the Test of Strength. Each orb must be hit countless times in a very short time period in order to destroy it.

THE GREAT TOWER

BOSS BATTLE: DRAKOR

Fingers tired yet? If not, they soon will be! After destroying the spires, the CloudRunner drops Fox through the center of the Great Tower to the lava filled underground temple below. Although he is fortunate enough to land on a floating metal platform, his luck quickly runs out when he sees who's there to greet him. The ruler of Dragon Rock is an armor-clad Drakor with a high-powered gun.

This battle is much like the aboveground destruction of the spires in that Fox is flown around through the maze of passageways and debris while trying to blast away at a moving target. In this case, the target is Drakor. Fox's only action is to hit Drakor enough times with the Fire Blaster to eventually destroy him. Fox has no way of controlling where Drakor or his metal platform flies and is essentially at the their mercy.

Although defeating Drakor is Fox's number one priority, and is where most of Fox's firepower should be aimed, some effort has to be put towards ensuring Fox's survival—this is a battle after all! For starters, Drakor has two attacks: the first a blue ray of energy similar to the Fire Blaster, and the other is a spiked metal bomb that hovers in place. Fox needs to make sure to blast the spiked metal

bombs with the Fire Blaster before colliding into them, else he'll suffer two blocks of damage. Also, it is possible to deflect the blue energy blasts by hitting them with the Fire Blaster. However, many of these shots sail wide of Fox anyway, it's often best to risk being hit and continue shooting Drakor.

138

Drakor and his attacks shouldn't be all Fox focuses on. Scattered throughout this underground gauntlet are numerous Special Crates (just like the ones encountered in space) that, when shot, award Fox with a Silver Ring. Obtaining a Silver Ring replenishes one block of energy. Shooting all of the Special Crates that appear is one way of ensuring Fox's survival in this seemingly endless war of attrition.

Finally, Fox must also be on the lookout for the orange panels mounted by the flame jets. Fox can shoot these panels to turn the flames off in time to pass through unscathed. Not every flame jet has a corresponding orange panel, but those that will do the most damage to Fox do have them.

Up Close and Personal — TIP

There are a few instances during the chase that Fox and Drakor will be practically right on top of each other. Take advantage of these times and blast away at Drakor's chest as fast as possible, even if it means getting hit with flames or bombs; a tremendous amount of damage can be done to Drakor when facing him. Don't let the opportunity pass by.

Once Drakor is defeated and laying at the bottom of the Great Tower, Fox will be able to return to the Ocean Force Point Temple with the final SpellStone. The dinosaurs that all chipped in to help Fox battle through the tests at Dragon Rock will all turn out to send him and Tricky on their way. As for them, they will happily await the moment that Dinosaur Planet is reassembled.

NOTE — Flying Home

The flight back to Dinosaur Planet is always the same: no Fuel Cells are consumed and the Arwing only needs to be flown through 1 Gold Ring to open the Force Field. See the first *ThornTail Hollow* chapter for tips on Gold Ring location.

DELIVERING THE FOURTH SPELLSTONE

CAPE CLAW

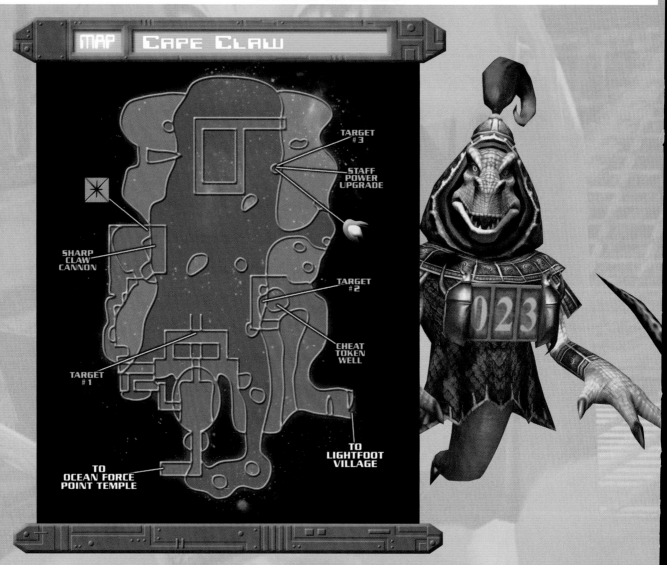

Swim across to the southwestern beach and enter the cave leading to the Portal. Use the Portal Device to open the door and extinguish the flame on the other side with the **Ice Blast**. Approach the SharpClaw Cannon and press the Ⓐ Button to start firing.

There are three targets here in Cape Claw that need to be demolished, and none of them are all that obvious.

1 For starters, turn the Cannon to the right and blast apart the boards the block the path to the Ocean Force Point Temple.

2 Rotate the Cannon to the left until it is just past the palm tree. Lob a cannonball at the rock wall under the trail leading back up the hill towards LightFoot Village. This will reveal a cave with the secret **Cheat Token Well** inside it.

3 Swing the Cannon towards the HighTop and use it to blow apart the rock outcropping between the HighTop and the northeastern beach. Buried in the rubble, Fox will find **BafomDad** and an entrance to an underground power-up location. Dive down the hole to gain the final **Staff Power** upgrade.

OCEAN FORCE POINT TEMPLE PART 1

MAP   Ocean Force Point Temple [Upper]

TO
CAPE-CLAW

ELECTRIC
FLOOR PUZZLE

CHEAT
TOKEN
WELL

TO
OCEAN FORCE
POINT TEMPLE
(LOWER)

Descend into the Temple through the narrow corridor and approach the electric floor puzzle. The way in which the puzzle is solved hasn't changed since Fox's first trip here. What has changed, however, is that the grid has expanded to nine rows of electrified panels instead of just six. This difference only necessitates more time being spent disarming the system.

Once again, an enormous SharpClaw patrols the far end of the hall. Defeat him with the freeze-n-slash technique and swim across the hall on the right. Use the Portal Device to open the sealed door to reveal another **Cheat Token Well**. Exit the room and use the warp pad atop the upper platform to enter the lower area of the Temple.

MAP   OCEAN FORCE POINT TEMPLE [LOWER]

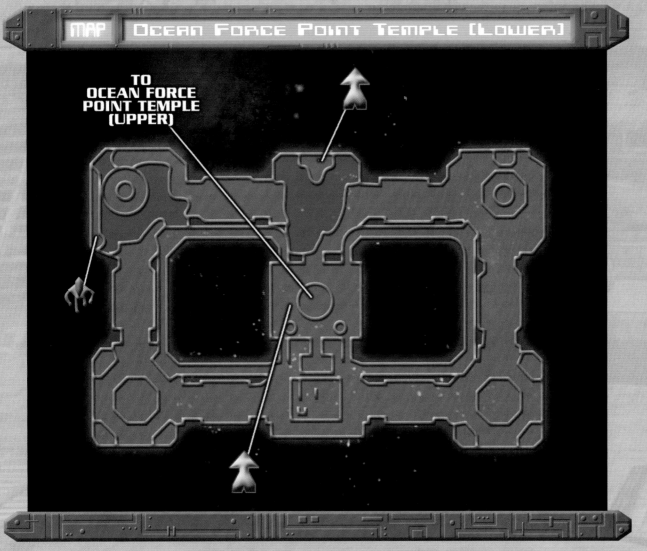

TO
OCEAN FORCE
POINT TEMPLE
(UPPER)

Fox's second trip to the lower area of Ocean Force Point Temple will require him to navigate the western rooms, as the puzzles in the eastern rooms have already been completed.

NORTHWEST ROOM PUZZLE

Push the large stone block to the north and use it to help Fox climb up to the ledge there. Flip the switch atop this ledge to open the door leading south. Jump across to the ledge near the Magical Plant and smash open the SharpClaw Crate to reveal a SharpClaw Pad. Don the SharpClaw Disguise and stand atop the Pad to reveal a secret switch in the side of the tower. Jump over and flip the switch to raise the water level in the room. Now Fox can swim southward to the next puzzle.

SOUTHWEST ROOM PUZZLE

The puzzle in this room is very similar to the one encountered in the southeastern room during the original trip to the Temple. Once again, a large central platform will rotate in a circle and Fox must trigger the Krazoa statues to bend over and blow the flames on the platform out. The catch is that this time the flames are four different colors and can only be extinguished by the Krazoa statue with the matching color.

Fox will have 3:00 from the time he flips the switch on the wall to extinguish all four flames. The best way to approach this task is to focus on just one single color at a time and keep the crosshair trained on one Krazoa statue. Anticipate the arrival of the flame and shoot the orange panel well ahead of time. Timing becomes even more critical after some of the flames have been extinguished, as the central platform will begin rotating much faster. By the time there are only two flames left, the platform won't even stop under the flame's corresponding statue but once every third rotation. Remember, the faster the flames are moving, the earlier the Krazoa statue must be triggered!

NOTE   GET OFF TO A GOOD START

Since the central platform increases in speed as each successive flame is blown out, it's important to not take too long putting out the first two flames. Consider flipping the switch and starting over if it takes over 2:00 to extinguish the first two flames.

SOUTH CENTRAL ROOM PUZZLE

This puzzle's mechanics are exactly the same as they were during Fox's earlier trip here. The only thing that has changed is the puzzles layout. The following directions detail the directions in which the crate must be "pushed" to reach the goal:

1:	West	5:	East
2:	North	6:	North
3:	West	7:	West
4:	South		

Once the puzzle is completed, the Rocket Boost Pad in the central room will become active. Rush back to the center room and Rocket up to the balcony above.

OCEAN FORCE POINT TEMPLE PART 2

There's only way to go once Fox is on the narrow balcony. Follow the path in a clockwise direction to the northwest room and fire a shot from the Fire Blaster through the flame and into the orb in the upper corner. Wait for the flame to change to the same color as the orb and then cross to the warp pad on the bridge that appears.

Much to Fox's dismay, placing the fourth SpellStone doesn't fully solve the problem of Dinosaur Planet's breakup. The various worlds continue to pull apart from Dinosaur Planet. Just as Fox smacks his head in disbelief, Peppy Hare pipes up over the radio to let Fox know that he's discovered a Krazoa Shrine entrance atop the large temple in the Walled City. Fox must return to the Arwing; it's time for a second trip to the Walled City.

REASSEMBLING DINOSAUR PLANET

WALLED CITY

Queen EarthWalker is waiting by the entrance to ThornTail Hollow and reminds Fox that her husband, King EarthWalker, still hasn't returned. The Queen believes that there is something at Walled City that's preventing it from reuniting with the rest of the planet. Rush back to the Arwing and make the journey back to Walled City at once!

NOTE **All the Better to See You With!**

Fox is going to need the magnification power of the **Hi-Def Display** to complete the puzzles at Walled City, so make sure to purchase them from the ShopKeeper if you hadn't already.

NOTE **Familiar Flight**

The flight back to Walled City is the same as it was during Fox's first trip there. Not only are the Gold Rings in the same locations, but the Arwing won't consume any more Fuel Cells either. See the *SpellStone #3* chapter for tips on Gold Ring location.

FINDING THE MOON STONE

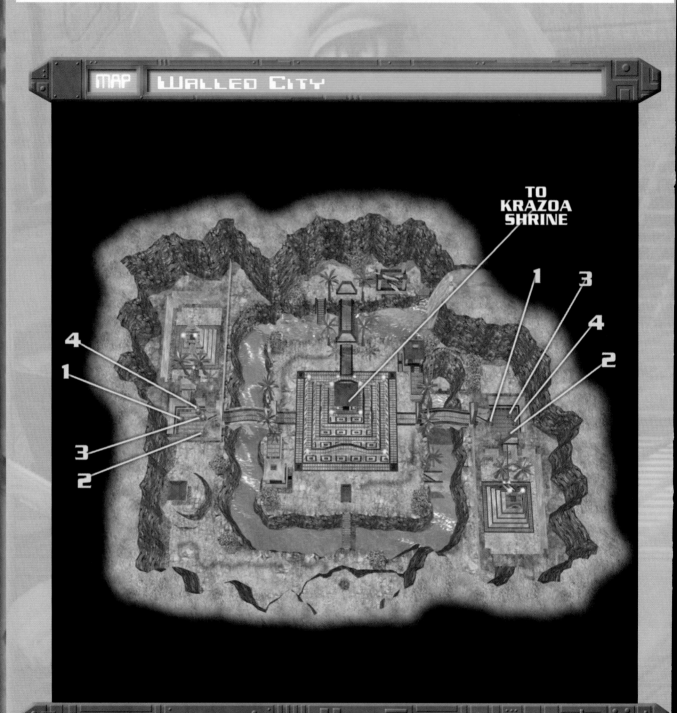

MAP WALLED CITY

TO
KRAZOA
SHRINE

146

Fox will find the King waiting for him on the steps of the main temple and he'll give Fox some important advice: Fox must return the Sun and Moon Stones to the temple if he wants to meet the Krazoa.

Cross the bridge on the eastern side of the Walled City to enter the Moon area. Fox is immediately met with a large puzzle consisting of four blocks inside of a grid. There are four lit squares that these blocks must be slid into. Like the floating crate at Ocean Force Point Temple, the blocks will reset if slid against the outer walls of the grid. The blocks can be slid into one another, however.

To solve the puzzle:

1:	Block 1 to the south (locked).
2:	Block 2 to the west.
3:	Block 3 to the south (locked).
4:	Block 4 to the west (locked).
5:	Block 2 to the north.
6:	Block 2 to the east (locked).

Once the puzzle has been solved, ride the angled lift to the top of the temple and peer through the circular hole at the tablet in the distance. Press the ⬤ Button to give the tablet a look through the Hi-Def Display and zoom in 100%. Staring into such light overwhelms Fox and he is forced to recoil from the brightness. It was for a good cause, however, as the passage leading into the basement of the temple has been opened.

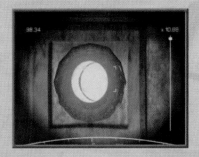

The first room in the temple contains what at first seems to be a rudimentary puzzle-flip the switch to open the door on the other end and wait for the gates to lower to cross. And then Fox notices that the panels in the floor fall away into depths below should he stand on one for over 2 seconds. Wait for the first gate to lower and then run across to the second area of floor panels. Utilize the panels off to the side to buy some time while waiting for the gate to lower. Step onto a panel, wait a second or so, and then quickly step to the next panel. Sprint to the third section and repeat this technique while zigzagging across the panels, only stopping on each for a second at a time.

WARNING SIGNS   TIP

The floor panel will lightly shake right before it breaks loose and plummets to the abyss below. Let this be your warning to quickly step off onto a safer panel. Try to avoid staying in one place so long, as you could inadvertently back yourself into a corner.

Once Fox makes it past the gates and over the breakaway flooring, he'll descend into a rather large room with just a circle of light on the floor. Perform a Super Ground Quake inside the lights to open the door to the south and to start the timer. Fox has 0:35 to navigate a mystical invisible maze (it will sparkle as he nears the walls).

To beat the timer, head off to the southwest corner and loop in a clockwise direction back along the perimeter to the northeast corner. Snake southward along the eastern wall back past the circle of light and out the door to the next room.

Use the Portal Device to unlock the seal leading deeper into the temple. Inside the next room is a wheel with a hole in it spinning in front of three switches. Fox must use the Fire Blaster to shoot the switches through the hole. Don't just start blasting though, Fox must shoot the switch next to the pictures of the quarter moon first (9 o'clock position), the half moon second (12 o'clock position), and lastly the full moon (3 o'clock position).

Once the three phases of the sun are lit, a cloudy pathway will bridge the gap, allowing Fox to take the Moon Stone from the center of the wheel.

148

FINDING THE SUN STONE

MAP | WALLED CITY

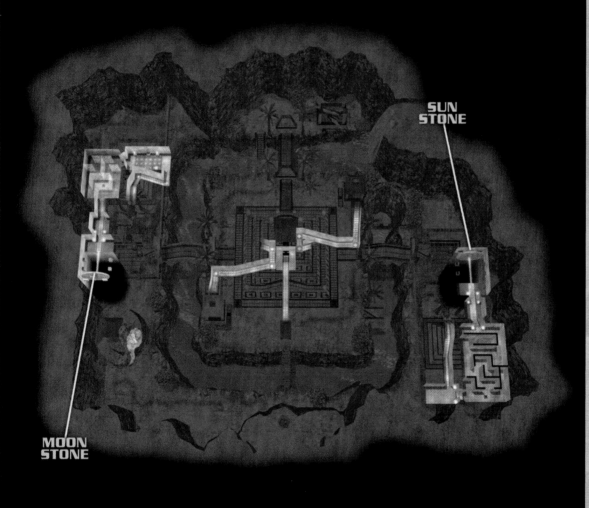

SUN
STONE

MOON
STONE

Cross the eastern bridge to the sun area and inspect the block puzzle. The mechanics of this puzzle are the same as the one in the moon area, however this one is slightly tougher to crack.

To solve the puzzle:

1:	Block 1 to the south (locked).	4:	Block 3 to the east (locked).
2:	Block 2 to the west.	5:	Block 4 to the west.
3:	Block 2 to the north (locked).	6:	Block 4 to the north (locked).

Once the puzzle has been completed, head to the top of the nearby temple and use the Hi-Def Display to zoom in on the sun tablet in the distance. Once Fox zooms in as close as possible, an underground passage into the temple will appear.

Use the Ice Blast to slay the flaming bats in the tomb below. Fox is faced with another, albeit less complex, puzzle. Each of the three wooden crates has a depiction of the sun or moon on one side. Pull each of the three blocks out and use the T-intersection to juggle their locations. Rearrange them so that the picture on each is facing into the room.

Head through the door that opens to the maze up ahead. Here, Fox must perform a Super Ground Quake inside the circle of light to start the clock. At that point, he'll have 1:20 to flip 4 switches inside the maze before time runs out. The switches must be flipped in order, though, as they will turn off invisible walls that block many of the routes through the maze.

Consult the accompanying map for switch locations.

1 Head west from the starting point to Switch #1.

2 Switch #2 is in the center of the maze. Extinguish the flame with the Ice Blast before trying to reach it.

150

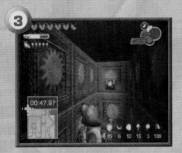

3 Head to the northwestern corner of the maze and shoot Switch #3 from across the gap with the Fire Blaster.

4 Switch #4 is behind the briars along the eastern wall of the maze. Have Tricky set flame to the prickly weeds and then flip the switch. Race through the exit to the north before the time expires to complete the maze.

Use the Portal Device to unlock the seal leading to the next room. Inside is a wheel with a hole in it spinning in front of three switches. Fox must use the Fire Blaster to shoot the switches through the hole. Don't just start blasting though, Fox must shoot the switch next to the pictures of the rising sun first (9 o'clock position), the midday sun second (12 o'clock position), and lastly the setting sun (3 o'clock position).

Once the three phases of the sun are lit, a cloudy pathway will bridge the gap, allowing Fox to take the **Sun Stone** from the center of the wheel.

RETURNING THE STONES

With both the Moon Stone and the Sun Stone in his possession, Fox is ready to unlock the entrance warp to the next Krazoa Shrine. Return to the tomb under the main temple where Fox had earlier set the Sacred Teeth. Place the Sun Stone in the center of the dragon statue on the left and the Moon Stone on the statue to the right. With the Stones firmly in place, a path to the top of the temple will appear, thereby giving Fox access to the entrance warp on the top.

KRAZOA TEST

1 Step onto the black panel in the floor to open the gate at the far end and then jump into the updrafts created by the fans. Don't worry about Fox's health; he has more than enough Energy Badges to withstand a couple of flames.

2 Float across to the central ledge and extinguish the flames there with the Ice Blast. Turn around and shoot the orange panel near the ceiling with the Fire Blaster to open the gate.

3 This room is just like the first, only the flames are spinning around a pair of platforms that Fox must run across. Ignore the flames and just cross the hall to the gate.

The Krazoa Spirit's Test of Knowledge consists of matching 6 items with the lands Fox had used them in. Fox will have 1:18 to complete this test. Each time an item is placed in front of the correct level, a large flame will erupt. Should the flame not appear, press the Ⓐ Button to pick up the item and try another level.

The following item/level pairings are in a counter-clockwise order starting with the area to the right of the entrance.

1 Place the **CloudRunner Flute** in front of the large marble dome.

2 Deliver the **Wood Block Carving** to the LightFoot hut.

3 Take the **Moon Seed** to the image of the crater in the cave.

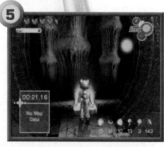

4 Take the **Gold Dragon Tooth** to the image of the temple in Walled City.

5 Place the **Dinosaur Horn** in front of the three stone columns.

6 Deliver the **Asteroid** to the image of outer space.

BEAT THE CLOCK   TIP

Since the six items are spread out in a wide circle, a lot of time can be wasted just running around. To finish this test with time to spare, place the items in the following order:

1	Gold Dragon Tooth	4	Moon Seed
2	CloudRunner Flute	5	Wooden Block Carving
3	Asteroid	6	Dinosaur Horn

NOTE   FLYING HOME

The flight back to Dinosaur Planet is always the same: no Fuel Cells are consumed and the Arwing only needs to be flown through 1 Gold Ring to open the Force Field. See the first *ThornTail Hollow* chapter for tips on Gold Ring location.

KRAZOA PALACE

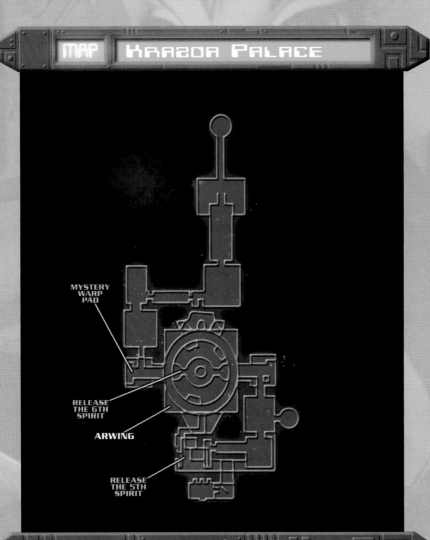

MAP **KRAZOA PALACE**

MYSTERY
WARP
PAD

RELEASE
THE 6TH
SPIRIT

ARWING

RELEASE
THE 5TH
SPIRIT

Fox will set the Arwing down on the roof of Krazoa Palace. Jump out of the ship and head to the north end of the Palace. Drop through the hole in the roof to the inside of the Palace and ride the wind lifts down one level to the third tier of the Palace.

Circle around to the corridor at the south end and float across the gap to the other side. Defeat the SharpClaw waiting in the large room at the end and step atop the glowing panel to release the fifth Krazoa Spirit.

Return to the rooftop of the Palace and head west along the rooftop to the warp pad that has since appeared. Fox will warp to a place foreign to him and a Life-Force Door will appear behind him as he arrives. Fox must defeat one enemy in order to remove the seal of the Life-Force Door.

THE FINAL KRAZOA SPIRIT

Climb the ladder and step into the sunlight in the center of the room to reveal the bearer of the sixth and final Krazoa Spirit—General Scales! Although it at first appears seems as though an epic battle is about to ensue, a familiar voice suddenly calls out to General Scales and demands he yield to Fox.

Surprisingly, the General does as he's told and surrenders the sixth Krazoa Spirit to Fox. Fox will automatically warp back to the rooftop. Walk due east towards the glowing panel and press the Ⓐ Button to release the final Krazoa Spirit.

155

SECRETS

CHEAT TOKEN WELLS

Dinosaur Planet contains eight Cheat Token Wells that, according to legend, award special powers to those who purchase a Cheat Token from their depths. Although the locations of these hidden wells have been discovered, their powers remain untapped. **Cheat Tokens** cost 20 Scarabs apiece. The Cheat Token Wells can be found in the following locations on the following page.

GAME WELL MAZE

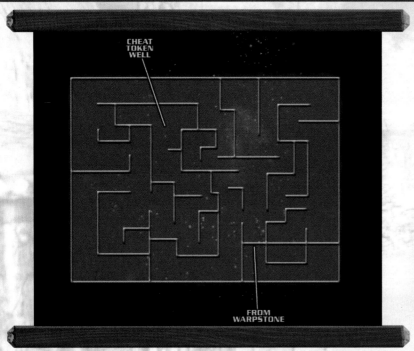

CHEAT TOKEN WELL

FROM WARPSTONE

Pay the WarpStone a visit and choose what's behind door number two to travel to the Game Well Maze. The maze contains several warp pads that lead right back to the WarpStone, but it also contains the first Cheat Token Well.

SECRETS OF THE CHEAT TOKENS

CHEAT TOKEN WELL	CHEAT OR FORTUNE
ThornTail Hollow Store	Display Credits Cheat
Ice Mountain	Play Tune Cheat (Plays all the music in the game)
SnowHorn Wastes	Fortune Told
Moon Mountain Pass	Dino Language (subtitles)
LightFoot Village	Fortune Told
Cape Claw	GFX Mode (semi Black & White)
Volcano Force Point Temple	Fortune Told
Ocean Force Point Temple	Fortune Told

ThornTail Hollow Store

This is the easiest Cheat Token Well to find since it's right in the middle of the floor.

Ice Mountain

Travel past the crates and the SharpClaw Cannon to the far end of the path and plant a Bomb Spore in the planting patch. Shoot the resulting plant with the Fire Blaster to blast your way into a cave containing a Cheat Token Well.

SnowHorn Wastes

Float all the way down the icy river to the eastern edge of the map to find the next Cheat Token Well.

Moon Mountain Pass

Traverse the pass towards the entrance warp leading to the Krazoa Shrine. Before reaching the Shrine, turn to the left and plant a Moonseed. Climb the vine up to the cave above to find a Cheat Token Well.

LightFoot Village

Return all three babies in the underground to their mother to have the Rocket Boost Pad near the gate activated. Rocket Boost onto the wall and run counter-clockwise towards the forest. Search the woods to the northeast to find the Cheat Token Well.

Cape Claw

Use the Cannon to blast the rock wall under the path leading up to LightFoot Village. The rocks will give way to a secret cave containing a Cheat Token Well.

Volcano Force Point Temple

Approach the left-hand ledge outside the main entrance to the Temple and climb down towards the lava. Plant a Moon Seed in the patch of grass near the wall and climb up to the small cave with the Cheat Token Well above.

Ocean Force Point Temple

Use the Portal Device to unlock the seal in the hall near the electric floor puzzle. There's a Cheat Token Well in the room beyond the seal.

TRICKY'S METAMORPHOSIS

Have you been playing fetch with Tricky as we told you to? Those who toss the ball around with Tricky whenever he asks will be treated to a colorful surprise—literally. Tricky will eventually change colors (and maybe more) from all of the extra exercise Fox has been giving him.

Star Fox® Adventures
Official Strategy Guide

Brady Publishing

An Imprint of Pearson Education
201 West 103rd Street
Indianapolis, Indiana 46290

ISBN: 0-7440-0122-6

Library of Congress Catalog No.: 2002111101

Printing Code: The rightmost double-digit number is the year of the book's printing; the rightmost single-digit number is the number of the book's printing. For example, 01-1 shows that the first printing of the book occurred in 2001.

05 04 03 02   4 3 2 1

Manufactured in the United States of America.

BradyGAMES Staff

Publisher
David Waybright

Editor-In-Chief
H. Leigh Davis

Creative Director
Robin Lasek

Marketing Manager
Janet Eshenour

Licensing Manager
Mike Degler

Assistant Marketing Manager
Susie Nieman

Credits

Project Editor
Christian Sumner

Screenshot Editor
Michael Owen

Book Designer
Kurt Owens

Production Designer
Bob Klunder

Maps By:
Idea + Design Works, LLC
www.ideaanddesignworks.com